ELZA SOARES

musical // *trajectories*

ELZA SOARES

ESSAY
Sergio Cohn

INTERVIEW
Ana Paula Simonaci
Leonardo Lichote
Paulo Almeida
Sergio Cohn (FINAL EDITION)

THE INVISIBLE BRIDGE COLLECTIVE

BACKLANDSPRESS oca
andantes LESMOTS
MOBILES

Musical Trajectory | Elza Soares

SERIES EDITOR AND GRAPHIC DESIGN
Sergio Cohn

TRANSLATION
The Invisible Bridge Collective
Darien Lamen

THE MUSIC TRAJECTORIES SERIES WERE ORIGINALLY CREATED BY
Ana Paula Simonaci | Janaína Marquesini | Leonardo Lichote
Paulo Almeida | Sergio Cohn

PHOTOS
Daryan Dornelles (cover, 14); Manchete archive (18, 23, 26, 31); O Cruzeiro archive (34);
Personal archive (40, 59); Sebastião Barbosa (51); Sergio Cohn (64); O Globo archive (72).

ISBN: 978-989-35445-7-0

THE INVISIBLE BRIDGE COLLECTIVE

OCA EDITORIAL (PORTUGAL, BRAZIL AND ANGOLA)
EDICIONES ANDANTES (SPAIN AND LATIN AMERICA)
LES MOTS MOBILES (FRANCE, BELGIUM AND CANADA)
BACKLANDS PRESS (USA, CANADA, UNITED KINGDOM, SOUTH AFRICA, JAPAN AND AUSTRALIA)

MORE THAN PUBLISHING HOUSES, BRIDGES BETWEEN CULTURES

musical / trajectories

The voices of the world are multiples, just as the ways people perceive themselves. While modern Western culture has predominantly evolved through philosophical and literary contemplation, emphasizing the written word, we cannot disregard the profound influence of music and spoken or sung words, even in these cultures. Music serves not only as a mode of expression but also as a fountainhead of thought. Numerous countries, especially in Africa and Latin America, fundamentally shape their thinking through music, though this phenomenon extends beyond these regions. Over recent decades, music has played a pivotal role in major social changes, firmly establishing itself as a vital instrument for transformation.

Through a blend of biographical essays, interviews, and discographies featuring prominent figures in world music, the Trajetórias Musicais collection offers a flavorful exploration not only into the history of contemporary music but also into significant political and social moments that have reshaped the world.

Published by The Invisible Bridge, a collective of publishers, artists, researchers and translators from different languages and countries – Oca (Portuguese), Andantes (Spanish), Les Mots Mobiles (French) and Backlands Press (English), with the intention of building bridges and dialogues between these cultures, the Trajetórias Musicais collection aspires to be more than just a series of books; it aims to be a political gesture fostering connection and openness to others, promoting candid dialogue, and building relationships between cultures. This endeavor is rooted in the belief that music serves as a vehicle for knowledge, cultural appreciation, and social transformation.

Introduction

Elza Soares (1937-2022) was what some contemporary feminists might call a space invader. Time and again, she used her wits, skills, and charm to stand her ground in hostile social spaces. In the process, she not only succeeded in supporting her family and pursuing her calling as an artist. She also created space for others, challenging the sexism, racism, and classism present in Brazilian society at large.

It's a truth we see reflected in many of the episodes that are recounted in this volume of Music Portraits, often in the artist's own words. During her first radio performance in 1953, for example, a young Elza famously took the stage next to host Ary Barroso – the composer of the internationally-famous song "Aquarela do Brasil" and one of the most revered Brazilian songwriters of the time – and turned his trademark condescension into a launchpad for her nearly 70 year career. "What planet did you come from?" Barroso had asked, to the amusement of the studio audience. "From the same planet as you, Mr. Ary," she responded. "Planet Hunger."

If Elza's modest clothing and dark skin had marked her as an outsider in that exclusionary space, her life experiences as a poor woman of color enabled her to speak to the realities facing many, if not most, Brazilian people, fellow inhabitants of Planet Hunger. By the 1970s, Elza found herself in a better position to advocate for them within the hostile spaces of the music industry. This included supporting Black songwriters and bringing Black singers into the recording studio with her, despite frequent objections from the record label. Right up until the end of her life, she continued to be known for taking fearless public stances on issues polite society preferred to ignore, whether that was her own experience of domestic violence and racism, or others' experiences of homophobia and transphobia.

But as the essay "Making a Living Making Art" in this volume also indicates, Elza was a kind of space invader in the aesthetic sense as well. Over the course of her career, she transgressed existing barriers between musical genres and audiences. During the 1950s and 60s, she performed not only bossa nova and jazz, but also roots samba and pagode, turning in the 1970s in an even more Afro-centric direction. In the 1980s, she embraced and was embraced by the emergent Brazilian rock movement. And beginning in the 2000s, her albums began to push the boundaries of the pop song form itself, incorporating elements of experimental, noise, and electronic music. As she explained in the 2019 interview with Azougue that is included here, "I'm not a soft drink that needs a label."

Elza Soares left this planet on January 22, 2022, but she leaves behind an important legacy as both an artist and a space invader. With her singular voice, and with the authority of her lived experience, Elza Soares dared to challenge racism, misogyny, and social exclusion. She did so in the music industry, in society at large, and in the home. Throughout her career, Elza dared to name the many forms of hunger that are experienced not only in Brazil, but also in the United States and beyond – hunger for food and income, yes, but also hunger for sexual freedom, education, social inclusion, cultural pride, as well as art and beauty. With this English-language edition of Music Portraits, we hope to celebrate Elza's legacy while also attending to the hunger we perceive among our readers for greater understanding and inclusion across linguistic and cultural boundaries.

Darien Lamen, PhD
Azougue Press, US Editor

Opening Act

Elza Soares is the best Brazil. Not the Brazil of natural beauty (which she possesses), or of exuberant taste (which she has), or of opulence (which she boasts), or of mixture (which she embodies). All these things are enormously present in her and would warrant the foundation of a nation. But this isn't the country we're talking about here.

The best Brazil – which Elza represents like perhaps no other singer – is the one Caetano Veloso once outlined, with the economical precision of a popular songwriter, in lyrics that speak of samba: "Samba is the father of pleasure / Samba is the son of pain / The great transformative power."

Elza is the Brazil that turns pain into pleasure. The great transformative power. In her trajectory as a singer and as a woman, she

1. The colloquial Brazilian Portuguese expression "dura na queda" (hard on the fall) means obstinate, stubborn, and, depending on the context, tenacious, resistant, tough.

endured many lives' worth of pain. Hunger, racism, ostracism, death, sexual violence, literal and figurative falls. However, in her hands, in her back, in her mouth, in her legs, in her body, in her throat, in her skin, in her soul, all the pain becomes like the flower in the song "Dura na queda"[1], composed for her by Chico Buarque, who writes that "for those who know how to see, the flower is also an open wound".

Thus, in Elza (in the best Brazil), hunger is transmuted into strength; racism into an unequivocal affirmation of Black greatness; objectification into sexual energy shaped by the very subject of that volcanic libido; ostracism into a comeback; setbacks into divine scratches in the voice; death into eternity.

This Brazil and this artist are at the center of this edition of Music Portraits. It's increasingly important for us to look into our best mirror. Almost two decades ago, right after seeing Elza on stage at her *Do Cóccix Até o Pescoço* show, the singer Seu Jorge stated: "This woman has to be taught in schools, she's more important than Pedro Álvares Cabral" (the Portuguese explorer credited with "discovering" Brazil).

The discovery is always greater than the discoverer. Or rather, the land is always greater than the one who invades it.

Leonardo Lichote
Brazilian Journalist and Music Critic

MAKING A LIVING
MAKING ART

Sergio Cohn

My name is Elza. Elza da Conceição Soares. I'm 25 years old. Nobody would guess I'm 25 years old. And for good reason. Today, I'm a singer. But before that, I even took a bullet. I don't even like to think about it.

I'm a Carioca from Piedade,[1] the daughter of a washerwoman. I got married when I was 12 years old. With a veil, a bridal tiara, and everything else. Don't be surprised; people from the slums also get married like that. A mother of six children, I lost two, who died of hunger. I now have six children. Four of them mine and two adopted. There are four boys and two girls. The oldest is almost 14 years old already.

Even so, I'm on my own. I've been fighting since I was a girl – a terrible fight, against everything and everyone. At 14 years old, I was already working in a soap factory, as a laborer. Then I went to a factory that made brushes for floor buffers,

1. A person from Rio de Janeiro is known as a "carioca"; Piedade is a hillside shanty town located on Rio's north side.

then another that made electrical appliances, until I ended up at a mental hospital out in Engenho de Dentro, working in the kitchen. I never sold myself. I was always very healthy and I was always able to work [1963].

This is how Elza Soares introduced herself, in the first person, in a statement for the magazine *Cruzeiro* in May of 1962. Although she was already an established singer, she did not hide the traces of Planeta Fome – "Planet Hunger" – that would accompany her through life. During more than 60 years of artistic career, Elza always maintained her integrity, using her gravelly voice to say that which is silent, while also remaining open to change and to time. Her voice has enchanted several generations, including international figures such as Louis Armstrong, Ella Fitzgerald, and Astor Piazzolla. Her voice even led to her being named "singer of the millennium" by BBC Radio London in 1999.

Elza Gomes da Conceição was born in the Moça Bonita favela in Padre Miguel, a neighborhood in the North Zone of Rio de Janeiro, on June 23, 1937.[2] As a child she went to live in Rio's Água Santa neighborhood, where her childhood was marked by extreme poverty, but also by the freedom of being able to play in the street. Elza was, as she put it, "a pest." She liked playing

2. Some sources list Elza's birthday as 1930, but in keeping with the dates established in her authorized biography, we have opted to include 1937 here.

"boy games": spinning tops, shooting marbles, flying kites. As she recalled decades later in a 2008 interview during her *Beba-me* ("Drink Me") tour [2008]:

> *I still love to fly a kite. When I drive by and see a child flying a kite, I feel like asking if I can have a turn. I even end my show by flying a kite while singing "Rap da Felicidade" [Rap of Happiness]. I never liked girl games like playing house, aprons, dolls – those lifeless things that don't cry, that don't do anything. I always thought women needed to be free. To fight, to live, to love, to be happy, and to be free. I've embodied that idea since I was a girl.*

Elza knew what she was talking about when, as a 70-year-old, she sang those emblematic funk carioca[3] verses on stage: "*Eu só quero ser feliz / Andar tranquilamente na favela em que eu nasci / E poder me orgulhar / E ter a consciência de que pobre tem o seu lugar*" ("I just want to be happy / To walk at ease in the favela where I was born / And be able to take pride / And know that the poor have a place.") Her childhood and youth were colored by life in the favela. There, the ever-curious girl discovered her unique singing voice by lifting a water bucket: "It was because of

3. A genre of Brazilian popular music from Rio de Janeiro that draws on Afro-Brazilian maculelê rhythms and an electronic Miami bass aesthetic, featuring chanted (rapped) lyrics.

the bucket of water that I discovered my gravelly voice. I would pick up the bucket and make a groan, and I discovered that I could do that in music." Or maybe it was by listening to the raspy buzz of her favorite insect, the praying mantis. And that's how life was, and might have remained, if it hadn't been for an incident involving that same insect which led to her forced marriage at the age of 12 [1997]:

> *It was a horrible thing. My father forced me to marry Alaúrdes Soares, and for a stupid reason. I always went to Água Santa to take my father coffee at work at 2 p.m. One day I put the coffee pot on the ground and went into the woods to catch a praying mantis. Alaúrdes followed me. I didn't like that and we started fighting. My father didn't know why we were fighting and he decided I had to marry him. He thought Alaúrdes had taken advantage of me sexually. He forced this arranged marriage. But on our wedding night, I thought we were going to fly a kite, or play marbles. And when I saw that naked thing in front of me, I was horrified. So, I ran down the hill to my father's house, who lived on the lot down below. I had a nervous fever, and that night I ended up sleeping between my father and my mother. When my dad realized that I hadn't had sex with Alaúrdes, he realized what a stupid thing he had done and he was heartbroken. With respect to sex, it was painful and boring, a sacrifice.*

The marriage lasted until Alaúrdes' death from tuberculosis. Elza, already a widow at the age of 21, inherited only her husband's last name and their children. Coincidentally, it was because of her son's health problems that Elza began her musical career. The year was 1953 and, to get money for medical treatment, Elza decided to audition for "Calouros em Desfile"[4] ("New Talent on Parade"), a radio program hosted by Ary Barroso, the composer of the famous song "Aquarela do Brasil." Elza was still a teenager, but she impressed the studio audience with her voice. However, she had to face many difficulties first, as she herself explained [2019]:

> *One day I discovered I could sing. My oldest son João Carlos was dying, and I'd already lost two children. I didn't want to lose another one. I didn't have money to take care of my son and I heard on the radio that Ary Barroso's show had a cash prize. I didn't know how, but I knew I was going to get that prize! I signed up and they told me I needed to look pretty. But I didn't have any clothes or shoes, I had nothing! So I took my mother's clothes – she weighed 130 pounds – and I put them on. But I weighed 70 pounds, so you can imagine, right? I made adjustments with safety pins. Nowadays this is fashionable, right? Even Madonna does it now, but I was the one who started this style, alright? Safety pins are so me, it's an Elza thing!*

4. Popular talent show that premiered on Radio Tupi since 1937.

On my feet I put on a type of sandal we used to call "mom-my, I'm in deep shit" and off I went! When they called me in, I got up and walked onto the auditorium stage. The auditorium was packed, and everyone started laughing and mocking me. Mr. Ary called me over and asked, "What did you come here for?"

"I came to sing!"

"Tell me, what planet did you come from?"

"From the same planet as you, Mr. Ary."

"And which one is my planet?"

"Planet Hunger!"

Everyone who'd been laughing saw that I was serious, so they sat quietly. I sang the song "Lama" ["Mud"]. They didn't ring the gong, I won, I left with the prize, and my son is still alive today, thank God! Since then, I always carry a safety pin with me.

At the time, I thought that if I had food for my children, I wouldn't be hungry anymore. Time went by and I was still hungry. Hungry for culture, dignity, education, equality, and much more. I realized that hunger only changes its face, but it is endless. There's always an emptiness that we can't fill and maybe that's the reason for our existence.

Elza's success on Ary Barroso's program not only saved her son, it also jumpstarted her career. She began appearing on other programs and attracting public attention. In addition to performing on the radio, Elza also managed to carve out space in the world of live performances, first as a singer with the Garan

Bailes Orchestra, and later in the realm of revue theater, which was very popular at the time.

Within this sphere, Mercedes Baptista was a central figure. Mercedes was the first Black dancer to become part of the ballet of the Teatro Municipal of Rio de Janeiro. She was also the creator of an Afro-Brazilian ballet, inspired by the Afro-Brazilian religion of Candomblé. Elza met Baptista in 1958, as Mercedes was staging *É Tudo Juju-Fru-Fru* ("It's All Juju-Fru-Fru"), a musical by the Silva Filho Company at João Caetano Theater in downtown Rio de Janeiro. Elza joined the cast. That same year, she was invited to go with Mercedes' group, the Ballet Folclórico Mercedes Baptista, to Argentina, where they traveled by ship. The show featured choreography that Mercedes had developed from various Afro-Brazilian cultural forms: cafezal, mondongô, samba, frevo, among other musical traditions. Elza Soares accompanied the group as a singer.

Their performances were very well-received in Argentina. But the manager, Ramon Shelber, who had invited the group on tour, disappeared with the money, leaving Mercedes unable to pay for the costs of the trip. With the assistance of the Brazilian embassy and theater critic Paschoal Carlos Magno, Mercedes managed to return to Brazil, but the rest of the team stayed behind. Elza Soares began singing in nightclubs to pay her bills and those of other musicians and dancers. According to Elza, the members of the group began to make their own way out of desperation: "The

girls tried to turn to 'the life' in order to make enough money to return to Brazil."

Despite all the difficulties, Elza later said that this period of apprenticeship in Argentina was of great importance in her life. Working as a "crooner" in nightclubs, she learned to perform various musical genres, developing a versatility that would accompany her throughout her career. In addition, she had the opportunity to play with important musicians such as Astor Piazzolla. According to Elza, when she met him, "Piazzolla was being heavily attacked. He was changing the tango, taking it out of that melancholic mode. He was doing a more modern tango and people didn't like it." The respect and friendship between the two would endure. Elza always said she was grateful for the opportunity that Mercedes Baptista presented her. It was a leap forward in her career and an experience that would help her become a performer with a broader repertoire.

Back in Brazil, Elza continued to perform on the radio before live studio audiences [1997]:

> *When I came back, I was lucky. I was invited to do a program on Rádio Mauá hosted by Hélio Ricardo, where the big singers as well as new ones performed. I also had a show on Rádio Mayrink Veiga that was written by Antônio Maria. My path started off rich! [The sambista] Moreira da Silva had heard me on Hélio Ricardo's program and asked him to become my godfather and take me to Aérton Perlingeiro's program on*

Rádio Tupi. It was a Sunday program, with Maestro Cipó's orchestra. My first experience on this program was fabulous, but at the same time very sad, because someone threw half a razor blade into my dress. I left the program to great applause, everyone was very happy, and I was even happier because I knew I was going to earn some money. I wasn't going to have to eat sardines with my kids anymore. Things were getting better. When I got back on the bus, a man told me I was bleeding. Then he found it and removed piece of razor blade. An angry female singer from Rádio Tupi had thrown that razor blade at me. After many years I met this singer's son and told him about it, and he was horrified.

Elza's encounter with samba artist Moreira da Silva was another one that would shape her professional life. Delighted by the voice he heard on the radio, Moreira had gone looking for her. He took her to Aérton Perlingeiro's show, then he convinced her to sing at the Texas Bar nightclub in Rio's upscale Leme neighborhood. They developed a solid and lasting friendship. Moreira da Silva was even the guarantor for Elza's first mortgage. As Elza herself put it, "The rogue could be trusted."

Her run of shows at the Texas Bar paid off. Elza attracted more and more attention, with musicians and producers beginning to follow her performances. Aldacir Louro, composer and promoter for RCA-Victor, was the first to take her to a meeting at a record company. But despite his enthusiasm for the singer he had dis-

ELZA Soares,
está com
fêz vibr
com o samba "N
no Meu
tantos os
(com   de Didi)
que a chamad Bossa egr
repetiu teu sucess

covered, negotiations with the record label didn't go forward. The reason was racial prejudice: although they perceived the potential of her voice, they thought a Black singer wouldn't sell. The fight against racism would be Elza's constant companion.

Nonetheless, Elza caught the attention of other producers, who realized she had the makings of a star talent. During one of Elza's performances, the singer Sylvinha Telles approached her and invited her to sit at her table and chat. Not recognizing the young bossa nova singer, Elza refused: "I came here to sing, not to sit at anyone's table." Accustomed to avoiding constant male harassment, Elza didn't understand what that "short woman with rabbit teeth" wanted with her. But Sylvinha introduced herself and convinced Elza to join the small group sitting together in the back of the club.

Some important figures in Brazilian popular music were gathered there, including bossa novista Roberto Menescal and Aloysio de Oliveira. In addition to being Sylvinha Telles' husband, Oliveira was one of the producers for the record label Odeon. He had been part of Bando da Lua, the group that accompanied Carmen Miranda in her North American career. He then became a key producer in the Brazilian music renaissance of the late 1950s and 60s, working first at Odeon before founding the record label Elenco, which released important records by musicians such as Vinicius de Moraes, Nara Leão, Dorival Caymmi and Edu Lobo, always with an emblematic cover in high contrast.

Aloysio invited Elza to record a single for Odeon, which she readily accepted. The recording session took place in a single afternoon in a packed studio, as the singer herself recalled in the beautiful 2018 biography *Elza* by Zeca Camargo [2018]:

> *[Radio singer] Lúcio Alves was there. Sylvinha Telles too, alongside her husband, Aloysio. Moreira da Silva watched me from afar, with a hint of pride. Even [bossa nova icon] João Gilberto went there to see me, which only made me more nervous. It seems Aloysio himself had spoken to [João] that morning, because he wanted him to hear this "cantora infernal" [diabolical singer] he had discovered and who had everything it took to succeed.*

Elza chose "Se Acaso Você Chegasse" ("If You Were to Come") by Lupicínio Rodrigues as her primary song. She'd already performed it in nightclubs and knew it worked. The recording included scat vocal improvisations that would make it famous. The scat was featured mainly in the chorus, but also in the instrumental part that takes up almost half of the recording of just over two minutes. The song, recorded in 1959, would become a major hit.

The excellent reception of the single led the label to release an LP with the same name the following year. In the text on the back cover, Elza introduces herself, reiterating her trajectory: "I'm 21 years old, I was a mother of six, I did a lot of time in the soap factory, and I sang in the little neighborhood club for a few bucks a session. If I hadn't been happy, what would have become of me?"

In addition to the title track, the LP featured songs such as "Mulata Assanhada," by Ataulfo Alves, and "Samba em Copa," by Cyro Monteiro. The last song on the album, "Não Quero Mais," was composed by Astor Silva, the trombonist who did the instrumental arrangements for this album and the following ones, *A Bossa Negra* (1961), *O Samba é Elza Soares* (1961) and *Sambossa* (1963). These records showed off Elza's singular way of singing. According to music critic Tarik de Souza [2016],

> *Like the jazz divas, Elza can both turn her voice into an instrument – now a hoarse trombone, now a strident electric guitar – and interpret the emotions in the lyrics to the point of making people laugh and cry according to the story of the song. In addition to her irresistible swing and precise phrasing worthy of Jackson do Pandeiro, she also excels in melodic themes. Her style of singing recalls Dalva de Oliveira's tortured vibrato and Angela Maria's sharp clarity.*

Elza's second album repeated the success of the previous one and became a landmark record. Produced by Ronaldo Bôscoli, a central figure of the bossa nova movement, the album is presented as follows in the liner notes: "The Black bossa of Elza Soares. Elza is the shantytown that went down to the highrise apartments, knocked on the rhythm door, and decided to live there." As Elza recalled [2016],

> *The record was born because of Ronaldo Bôscoli. At the time, he was writing for* Cruzeiro *magazine, and he thought I would be an important figure, a representative of the Black race, and he said: "This is what I'm looking for. You're going to be the representative that we searched so long for, and we're going to make an album called* A Bossa Negra *[The Black Bossa]." He wanted to turn me into a kind of Sarah Vaughan.*

At the same time, Bôscoli and Elza also decided to conduct a campaign to provoke high society and challenge racial prejudice [2016]:

> *We did several experiments. Ronaldo Bôscoli brought me to Copacabana Palace. He arranged for the handsomest guy at the time to accompany me so everyone would think he was my boyfriend. And when that beautiful Black man and I arrived together at the Copacabana Palace, nobody waited on us, nobody came near us. Then the television crew came in to find out why we weren't served. We did that at the Copacabana Palace, at Sacha's, and at Quintandinha too. And it was always the same story. The waiter would pass by, we would call him,*

5. A style of samba that frequently includes wind instruments in the line-up, and that is oriented toward dancehall or ballroom performance

and he would pretend not to see us. So Ronaldo developed this campaign to show the racism that we live with here in Brazil.

The first albums Bôscoli produced for Elza had a lively and fully-orchestrated *gafieira*[5] sound that highlighted the singer's raspy scat improvisations. According to Elza [2016],

> *They had a jazz orchestra, with a big band format. One day I was listening to Frank Sinatra, and I realized the arrangements were similar. All the arrangements by the conductor Nelsinho at the time had a lot in common with the arrangements by Sinatra, by Natalie Cole. But with a certain something different, with a different swing, because it had the rhythmic syncopation of samba.*

For Tarik de Souza, Elza and Bôscoli's albums were emblematic of the *sambalanço* style that was in evidence during that period [2016b]:

> *Not every change samba underwent from the 1950s to the 1960s can be classified as bossa nova. Although they didn't constitute an ideological or even a programmatic movement, several composers, musicians, and performers transformed the main Brazilian genre during this period to give it greater rhythmic impact and a new instrumental structure in an aesthetic process that became known as "sambalanço." Like the trend*

itself, the fuzzy label lacks sharpness. Among its shared features are the punctuation of the piano, the organ, and the early electric keyboards; the woodwinds with their more percussive inclination; and the accentuated rhythm pattern (sometimes with an Afro-Caribbean accent) that facilitate partner dancing. And verses which were almost always good-humored and overflowing with exaltation or with lyricism.

Even if Elza did not adopt bossa nova as her own style, her relationship with that movement was intimate. She would even go on to record some of the most famous bossa nova songs, such as "Dindi" and "Garota de Ipanema." She was also friends with some of its leading figures, including Tom Jobim and João Gilberto. She was particularly close to the latter, as she explained: "At that time João Gilberto was a good friend of mine. He used to go to my house to see how I divided my phrases, because he thought my melodic phrasing was crazy. We were truly friends. João Gilberto and I, Tom Jobim – those people really liked me."

With the positive response to her records by both critics and the public, Elza had become a phenomenon. Her widespread popularity led to her being invited to become "godmother" to the Brazilian national soccer team in 1962, the year it became two-time World Champion at the World Cup in Chile.

Elza flew to Chile and sang alongside Louis Armstrong. The great U.S. jazz singer was enchanted by that 5-foot-2-inch-tall woman who had, in his words, "a saxophone in her throat," and

he affectionately referred to her as his "daughter." But Elza, not understanding English, couldn't help but create a small controversy: "He called me 'daughter' and I thought he was saying 'doctor,' so I asked people to tell him that I wasn't a doctor at all, and that he could call me Elza. But they told me he was saying I was like a daughter to him, and that I should be nice and call him 'my father.' But it sounded like 'me fuder,' and I thought they saying he should fuck me, and I refused." Once the confusion was cleared up, Elza said there was nothing but mutual admiration for each other's gravelly voices and skill at improvisation: "Improvisation, this Black thing, was part of me even before I met any jazz musicians," Elza later said.

During the same year of 1962, Elza met Mané Garrincha – the star of the Brazilian national team and of the Rio de Janeiro-based soccer club Botafogo – who was known as "the joy of the people." The two became protagonists of a great love affair. In an interview with her friend Ronaldo Bôscoli in the 1980s, Elza recalled the story [1985]:

> *Once upon a time there was a fairy tale. The year was 1962 and there was a contest where the friendliest player on the national soccer team would win a car. I was Garrincha's campaign manager and he won. To repay the kindness, he managed to get a lot of rice for my house. There was rationing during this period. But he insisted on delivering the goods personally. It was unheard of! Beans and rice over here, beans and rice over*

there, and Garrincha ran into my heart like he ran past his opponents on the field. It left me stunned – that way of his I'll never forget. Our romance started out in secret. He'd had an affair with Angelita Martinez and he was terrified of scandals. As a matter of fact, he drank very little at the time – just a little liqueur as an aperitif.

It was 1962, the year I was hired by Edmundo Klinger to work in Chile, and I ended up becoming godmother to the [Brazilian national] team. The managers knew about Mané's sexual appetite and they were sympathetic. Without a good deal of the "horizontal plane" he didn't perform on the field. Can you believe he promised me a head goal during the finals against Chile and he delivered? Although I share it with Brazil, that goal is mine. When we returned home, we had a plan: we wouldn't live together. But the press forced us to. Do you know what it's like to have sex in hiding?

Their love affair would turn into a 17-year marriage, marked by the comings and goings of Garrincha's alcoholism. In Elza's words, the soccer star was "the most beautiful figure in the world, a child" while sober. But when he drank, he would transform. As Elza explained [1985]:

As long as the alcohol didn't cancel out Mané, we were very happy. Like in the movies. One of us looked at the other, and no matter what time it was, the sparks would fly. It was a

Elza and Garrincha's relationship was troubled from the start, with numerous attacks from the public and the press. They accused Elza of having stolen Garrincha from another woman, the mother of his children. Elza defended herself as best she could, as she did in the statement she gave to *Intervalo* magazine in August 1963:

I carry a lot of sadness, because I was never able to be a girl like the others, I was never able to be a woman like the others. Now that I want to be a woman, I'm finding it very difficult. I don't know, but it seems like everything I do doesn't work out, because I hear a lot of criticism from this immense beloved public that made me an international singer. I love my public, and I live from it and for it. But I also need to live for myself, for this great love that I've found, and for my children. The people who've been attacking me don't know that our golden dream – mine and Manoel's – is to be parents to both my sons and his daughters. Both of us are affectionate. Both of us are loving and we want the same for our eleven children. The rest is a separate issue. Both of us were unhappy in marriage. Both of us got married before adulthood, without knowing what we were doing. We were victims of fate in the same way. Maybe

While the constant criticism saddened Elza, she remained firm and gained more and more recognition for her music.

In 1967, she began a professional partnership with the singer Miltinho that yielded a three-volume album entitled *Elza, Miltinho e Samba*. Miltinho was already a successful singer when they started their artistic partnership. He'd participated in mainstream samba ensembles such as Anjos do Inferno and Quatro Azes e Um Coringa. Like Elza, Miltinho had been a winning participant on Ary Barroso's radio show with his vocal group Cancioneiros do Ar. In addition to being a singer, Miltinho was a great rhythmist. As he proudly noted: "In my day, a pandeiro player didn't sing. I was the first one." Miltinho became famous for his nasal voice and the rhythmic division of his vocals: "I'm a rhythmist. The only difference is that I sing two beats late, and the harmony goes ahead. You have two beats to make mistakes. People don't know that two beats in music is a neverending thing, you have time to write a letter home." According to the renowned sambista Martinho da Vila, Miltinho's self-confessed fan, "Miltinho had a lot of swing. His rhythm isn't easy to learn. It's a living thing. Today we don't have any singers with his style, with that syncopated samba division."

Elza and Miltinho's partnership was so fruitful that they performed three-hour-long live shows and were given their own TV program. Their albums featured delightful reinterpretations of classic sambas by Noel Rosa, Ismael Silva, Francisco Alves, João do Vale, among other major figures. In 1968, Elza released another wonderful album in partnership with another percussionist – the drummer Wilson das Neves. As she recalled [2016]:

> *We were in Buenos Aires doing a show, when a director for Odeon showed up. I asked him: "Don't you want to give me a present?" "What present?" "Can I make a record with Wilson das Neves?" "But I've never seen a singer who's a drummer…" "You'll see it for the first time!" From there, we went to Rio, chose the repertoire, and recorded it. It was a beautiful record. It seems like it was recorded yesterday, it's still so current. One of the songs, "Deixa Isso Pra Lá," could be considered as a precursor to rap – it's just voice and drums. And that was 1968!*

Elza was at her peak in the late 1960s. But life had new tragedies in store for her: her mother died in a car accident while Garrincha was behind the wheel. In addition, she and Garrincha were receiving increasingly violent threats [1997]:

> *We've received repeated threats by mail and phone saying we have to leave the country or die. They took our house. It was shot up with a machine gun and we left for Italy. I'd been playing with the children, and we started hearing gunfire. Botafogo [soccer club] sent a guard to take care of the house*

where we lived in the Jardim Botânico neighborhood. He was shot in the arm. I was completely terrified for the children. I had a piano in the living room, it was split in half.

In the early 1970s, Elza and Garrincha effectively decided to leave the country. After much hesitation, Elza had accepted invitations from the producer Franco Fontana to perform in Italy. They went to live in Rome, where they spent a season punctuated by achievements as well as great difficulties. The Brazilian songwriter and lyricist Chico Buarque was also living in Rome at the time with his wife, actress Marieta Severo. The couple not only became Elza and Garrincha's friends, but also fundamental emotional support, especially for Garrincha, who struggled with the change of environment. As Chico Buarque recalled [2019],

> *We became very good friends. We got together all the time. Obviously I used to talk about soccer – and him about music. It was the same with Pelé, who loves music. But Garrincha was very musical. I had more contact with him in Rome. Garrincha knew music much more than I'd imagined before. He liked João Gilberto. I imagined Garrincha would like simpler music perhaps. But no! Garrincha liked the sophistication of a João Gilberto.*
>
> *He commented on recordings, referred to details, remembering how João Gilberto sang a certain song. To show me, Garrincha hummed – not very well – but it demonstrated that*

he'd memorized João Gilberto's songs. He was referring to the way João Gilberto sang the songs. João is an inventor. Not a composer. Perhaps he is more than a composer, because he invents from someone else's music. And Garrincha would talk about that: the way João Gilberto sang – perhaps a well-known song that he had rerecorded, like "Aos Pés da Cruz." Garrincha highlighted the way João Gilberto reinvented a samba.

I was Garrincha's driver. He played a few games on the outskirts of Rome. He earned a fee for some of them. I was the one who drove Garrincha in my Fiat. It was impressive. People stopped in the street. Garrincha was very popular. This happened in 1970. Garrincha had already stopped playing for some time. Eight years had passed since the 1962 World Cup, but he was still very well-known in Italy.

Elza's debut in Italy was at the Teatro Sistina. It was a success: the audience filled the theater's 1500 seats and were ecstatic with the repertoire performed. It was the first in a season of shows that delighted Italian audiences. According to Elza [1997],

In Rome, we stayed in a beautiful apartment in Vila Bevagna, close to Corso di Francia. Things went well until 1971. I made a lot of money. I had a $60,000 semi-annual contract with Franco Fontana, one of the biggest Italian businessmen. And there were months when, in so-called piccoli presentations,

I earned almost half of the official contract. The press talked about me, and the Italians liked to hear me singing samba and showing that "mulata swing." Some shows turned into a party, with a lot of people trying to imitate my swing.

But it wasn't just the public that was enchanted by Elza. Ella Fitzgerald, the great American jazz singer, also became impressed with her voice. Ella was in the middle of a European tour performing songs by Tom Jobim when she had a medical problem and needed a replacement. Elza was chosen [2016]:

We met at a fancy restaurant in Rome. I don't know how it's possible that there's no photo of that night: myself, Ella, Jorge Ben, Trio Mocotó, Garrincha, and Franco Fontana were sitting at a table. Ella sought me out at the suggestion of Naná Vasconcelos, who was already an internationally-recognized percussionist. Ella needed cataract surgery and she was looking for a singer to replace her. Naná, who was friends with her, called and said I was the only one who could sing in her place. They showed her some records of mine and she loved it and wanted to meet me. I sang several shows, because her tour schedule was already full from the previous year. At first, people thought it was strange not finding Ella on stage. But when I started to sing, soon everyone was standing up applauding. It was wonderful!

Elza's stay in Europe was short-lived and the return to Brazil would be challenging. Elza wanted to reclaim her place in the music scene but she found out she had a strong competitor. Clara Nunes was Odeon's big bet at the moment. That particularly pained Elza, because they were friends. When people compared them to each other, Elza was forceful: "I was the one who launched Clara's career. I was the one who took her to Odeon. She came to me when she arrived from [the state of] Minas and wanted a reference. When they heard her sing, they hired her immediately. I was very happy because I was a dear friend. If there's some similarity, it's because someone else is similar to Elza."

This wasn't the only setback Elza would experience with Odeon upon her return from Italy. She wanted to make an album in partnership with a singer she had heard on the car radio, a man whose voice she found enchanting – Roberto Ribeiro. But the Odeon label was now in the hands of business executives, and not the devoted producers from before. When Elza first arrived at the record company in the late 1950s, the director at the time was André Midani, a towering figure in Brazilian music who supported innovative movements such as bossa nova and Tropicália. In the 1970s, it was a very different Odeon from the one she remembered. "For about six years and half a dozen LPs, Odeon and I were very happy. Maestro Astor, Ismael Côrrea, Milton Miranda, I don't know... It seemed like a big family," Elza recalled.

The new directors didn't understand why Elza wanted to record an album with an unknown singer, but Elza insisted on the project with the goal of reinventing not only her image but also her sound. To that end, she called on the pianist Dom Salvador to do the arrangements. One of the founders of samba-funk, Dom Salvador had recorded the wonderful album *Som, Sangue e Raça* the previous year with his band Abolição. Embracing Elza's vision for the project, Dom Salvador agreed and together, he, Elza, and Roberto Ribeiro created the LP *Sangue, Suor e Raça* [Blood, Sweat, and Race].

The first track, "Swing Negrão" [Black Swing], begins with verses Elza herself composed: *"Moreno vem cantar comigo / Eu fiz um samba / Para você sambar / Moreno vem cantar comigo / Eu fiz um samba / E só você pode cantar"* (*"Moreno* come sing with me / I made a samba / For you to dance to / *Moreno* come sing with me / I made a samba / And only you can sing it.") The message was clear: Elza had returned from her season abroad a different person, and she was ready to fight. For one thing, she not only insisted on including Roberto Ribeiro in the recordings, but also on the record cover. The record company resisted. Elza recalled [2016]:

> *Years later, when they made a documentary about Roberto Ribeiro, his family sought me out. They told me that the last thing he said before he died was "Elza defended me." And that's exactly right! When they wanted to take him off the cover, I tore up my contract in front of the label's board! Their argument was that Roberto was too ugly, but I knew it was racial*

prejudice. And I fought until the end, because if they wanted my record, it would have to be with him.

In the end, Elza triumphed and the record was a success. Odeon also became convinced that Roberto Ribeiro was a talent to be developed. He went on to have a solid career with them during the 1970s. But the episode led to a break between Elza and the label that had stood by her for nearly 15 years. In a conversation with Ronaldo Bôscoli, Elza recalled: "I thought that the English people [in charge of Odeon] were sabotaging Black folks. With me less so, but with Roberto Ribeiro the behavior was outrageous. So, I threw it all away."

That same year, Elza released one of the best albums of her career, *Elza Pede Passagem*, with arrangements once again by Dom Salvador. The album further aligns Elza's image with the movement for Black freedom and equality. On the cover, the singer appears with bell-bottoms and an afro. The repertoire is almost entirely samba, featuring compositions by a new generation of songwriters like João Nogueira, Gonzaguinha, Zé Rodrix, and Luiz Carlos Sá. Although these songwriters were already somewhat well-known by that time, their inclusion in the project reflected Elza's ever-present interest in lifting up new composers [2016]:

I love helping new composers get their start. You take people who are unknown and who sing, you get to uncover something new, and you also give the person a chance to do their work.

It's singing without selfishness. I've always had this concern. There always used to be a bunch of people standing around the entrance to the record company who would call out to me, "Elza, Elza, Elza!" And I didn't understand why [my handlers] were pulling me along, not letting me talk to those people. They were new songwriters who wanted an opportunity. The record company used to say it wasn't possible, it wasn't going to happen. So I'd invite them to my house, and they'd sing. On the day of the recording session, I'd take that little group of people with me. They used to call it my "slave ship" [navio negreiro].

It was prejudice, always present. "It's a little weird. When Elza sings, it looks like a slave ship." But I kept on. After all, I was part of that ship. I fought hard to include those song-writers. They'd say I shouldn't worry about them, because I already had a repertoire prepared, because I was "our Sarah Vaughan," "our Ella Fitzgerald." In the beginning, I used to ask myself: "What's that about?" I didn't even know what it meant. I thought, "What I want to know is when am I going to be Elza?" But the important thing then was to bring food home to my children.

Elza's new sound caught on in Brazil and abroad. With a new band comprised of top-notch musicians, she was able to complete a successful tour of North America [2016]:

I started to understand that it wasn't just drumming that I wanted. I wanted something funkier – samba soul, samba jazz. And at that time, I formed a band with Wilson das Neves, Dom Salvador, Nizo Barroso, and Geraldo Vespar. The name of the group was "Só Som," and we went to the United States first. I received a standing ovation, and when the show ended in New York, we went to Mexico. I was contacted by Sammy Davis Jr.'s secretary. He wanted to work with me at Motown, the Black record company. But Odeon prevented that from happening, because I still had a contract with them. I went back to Brazil and Dom Salvador stayed in the U.S., which was wonderful.

Back in Brazil, Elza would record one more album for Odeon before she switched record labels. It was arranged by Laércio de Freitas, the great pianist who worked with artists such as João Donato, Marcos Valle, and Wilson Simonal. She was then hired by the Brazilian label Tapecar, but it didn't turn out well for her there [1997]:

I got bad advice and went to Tapecar. I sold a ton of records and didn't earn anything. My hits had no financial return and I started to survive off of small shows accompanied by modest bands. I started going downhill. A quiet move to CBS and lots of crying in bed. The only reason I didn't do anything stupid,

Elza released four albums with Tapecar between 1974 and 1977,
the first three with arrangements by Ed Lincoln, an experienced
musician who also worked with samba singer Beth Carvalho.
Considered the "King of Bailes (Dances)," Ed Lincoln possessed
a rhythmic sensibility that allowed him to develop a contagious
sound characterized by African aesthetic elements.

In this way, Elza was able to compete with Clara Nunes, who
had become a huge success. On the cover of her first Tapecar
album, Elza appears wearing a white headwrap, which invited
further comparisons between her and Clara, who also styled
herself after the iconic figure of the Afro-Brazilian *baiana*.

But Elza's Tapecar records had a more irregular repertoire,
featuring songs by new composers (among them Jorge Aragão,
who would become Elza's musical godson). Although they were
popular, they removed Elza from the vanguard of Brazilian popular
music. Her fourth and final Tapecar album, *Pilão + Raça = Elza*,
embraces the rootsy samba subgenre of *partido alto*. In it, Elza
tried her hand as a composer of three songs: "Língua de Pilão,"
"Enredo da Piraça," and "Perdão." But in the end, the album was
not successful.

The late 1970s were very difficult for Elza. After having a child
with Garrincha, the couple decided to separate permanently
[1997]:

Unfortunately, Garrincha's biggest influence was alcohol, right up until his death. He got aggressive, and it got to the point where we had to split up. I still have marks on my body to this day. I did what I could. I even gave him a son, Garrinchinha, his love. When I got pregnant, I proposed a pact, an agreement. If it was a boy, we would separate. It was a way of controlling his alcoholism. I was tired of waiting up all night to wash his feet and feed him some broth out of a bottle. At the end of our relationship, he no longer ate anything. His only appetite was sexual... It's true that during my pregnancy, while we waited for Junior, Garrincha didn't touch alcohol. It seems like he stored it all up for the day his son was born. He ended up being admitted to a clinic. I think that was the first time. Three days after my delivery he showed up with a bouquet of flowers, even more wilted than he was. He was still drunk. He confessed, sobbing: "It's no use, it's stronger than me. I'm going to keep drinking." We parted ways.

Shows became infrequent. The financial constraints tightened. The albums Elza released on CBS – *Senhora da Terra* (1979) and *Elza Negra, Negra Elza* (1980) – had no purchase, despite their quality repertoire. Before long, Elza was performing as part of circuses, a source of sadness for an artist who had experienced so much national and international success. But she had her youngest son Garrinchinha to worry about, and she needed to support him.

On January 20, 1983, at the age of 49, Garrincha died. Elza decided to give up her career in music and work in childcare. That was the moment Brazilian singer Caetano Veloso offered to help, as Elza recalled in a conversation with Ronaldo Bôscoli entitled "Elza Soares' Comeback" [1985]:

> *An angel named Caetano Veloso has come into my life. I was feeling desperate about everything, and I looked him up in São Paulo. He received me with the greatest affection. "Look, Elza," Caetano told me, "after this show I'm going to take a short trip. Here's my address. Look me up." It was true. He invited me to sing on one of the tracks on his new album Velô called "Língua." And after that, there were a thousand interviews and lots of hype, and I was invited by Chico Recarey to record an album and do a show that Caetano himself named "Exagero." I was whole again. I owe my comeback to this Bahian boy named Caetano. This is my chance. I've got no more time to waste [1985].*

The distinctive sound of Elza's raspy voice singing the chorus of "Língua" ("Language/Tongue") would soon win over legions of new fans and revive old acquaintances: *"Flor do Lácio Sambódromo Lusamérica latim em pó / O que quer / O que pode esta língua?"* ("Flower of Lacio Sambadrome Powdered-Latin Luso-America / This tongue, what does it want / What can it do?") Elza resumed her career and was hired by the Som Livre record label to make a new album. In 1985, she released *Somos Todos Iguais*, which incorporated songs by renowned songwriters such as João Donato and Martinho da Vila (including the beautiful song "Daquele Amor, Nem Me Fale"), as well as songs by younger artists such as Cazuza and Frejat (for example, the impressive blues song "Milagres": *"A fome está em toda parte / Mas a gente come / Levando a vida na arte"* ("Hunger is everywhere / But we eat / Getting by with art"). The album's title track, a Cuban salsa in a 1980s arrangement, was composed by Elza herself. The album also includes an appearance by Caetano Veloso on "Sophisticated Lady," a version of the Duke Ellington classic adapted by the Brazilian poet Augusto de Campos.

The Brazilian music scene during the 1980s was characterized by the consolidation of national rock. Bands like Barão Vermelho, Titãs, Ira! and Paralamas do Sucesso took over radio and television programs. It was the moment of the first Rock In Rio festival, as well as of political redemocratization following Brazil's military dictatorship. The political opening allowed for the renewal of more cheerful, uncompromising attitudes in society and in music. Elza quickly joined in. She performed a series of shows called *A Vingança Será Maligna* [Revenge Will Be Evil] with the rock band Titãs at the legendary Madame Satã nightclub in São Paulo. She appeared on the TV show "Fantástico" singing a duet of the song "Milagres" with Cazuza. She recorded a new version of her first ever 1959 single "Se Acaso Você Chegasse" with rock artist Lobão. A younger generation fell in love with her energy [2016]:

I was crazy. I remember they said at the time: "This crazy woman – I don't know how she does it! She mixes samba with jazz, she mixes it with funk, with rock, she mixes everything!" At one time in the 1980s, I was a rocker in São Paulo. I dyed my hair all white. The next day it all fell out, but it didn't matter. I played Madame Satan with the Titãs. All the young people were with me. When Elza Soares took the stage, I had to stop because the floor of the house started to sink. It was crazy!

Things seemed to be getting back on track, but life would bring more sad surprises. In 1986, when Elza seemed to have been reborn into music, her youngest son died in a car accident. He had gone to visit the grave of his father, Garrincha. He was nine years old. Devastated, Elza left everything behind and went to live abroad [1997b].

| 54

When my son died, I totally lost control. I dropped everything and left for America, completely alone. I was very upset. I spent years traveling, without finding anywhere I wanted to be besides Brazil. I don't believe there's anyone more patriotic than me. I'm almost gross about it. I looked at Paris and said: "It doesn't look like Brazil." I went to London: "London is gray." New York: "No, I don't like it."

Only after eleven years did Elza finally return to Brazil. And she was welcomed home with open arms. With a repertoire of songs by big names in Brazilian music such as Chico Buarque, Guinga, Aldir Blanc, and Nei Lopes, she recorded the beautiful album *Trajetória* with a special guest appearance by samba artist Zeca Pagodinho. The album includes more traditional samba repertoire and arrangements, as well as a sophisticated performance by Elza. The response from critics and audiences was immediate. Elza's career picked back up at a high level. She resumed an intense schedule of concerts and was celebrated as one of the great names in Brazilian music. In 1999, BBC Radio London named her "Singer of the Millennium," consolidating her international reputation.

But that same year, Elza took a tumble off the stage during a show at the performance venue Metropolitan, in Rio de Janeiro. She fell from a height of about six feet and suffered spinal cord compression in her lower back. But still she persisted. In an homage to her incredible resilience, Elza's friend Chico Buarque wrote the song "Dura na Queda," which became one of the main songs in her repertoire:

Perdida / Na avenida / Canta seu enredo / Fora do carnaval / Perdeu a saia / Perdeu o emprego / Desfila natural // Esquinas / Mil buzinas / Imagina orquestras / Samba no chafariz / Viva a folia / A dor não presta / Felicidade, sim // O sol ensolará a estrada dela / A lua alumiará o mar / A vida é bela / O sol, estrada amarela / E as ondas, as ondas, as ondas, as ondas // Bambeia / Cambaleia / É dura na queda / Custa a cair em si / Largou a família / Bebeu veneno / E vai morrer de rir // Vagueia / Devaneia / Já apanhou à beça / Mas para quem sabe olhar / A flor também é / Ferida aberta / E não se vê chorar / O sol ensolará a estrada dela / A lua alumiará o mar / A vida é bela / O sol, estrada amarela / E as ondas, as ondas, as ondas, as ondas.

Lost / On the avenue / She sings her story / Outside carnival / She lost her skirt / Lost her job / She struts along naturally // Street corners / A thousand honking horns / She imagines orchestras / Samba at the fountain / Long live revelry / Pain's no good / Happiness, yes // The sun will shine on her road / The moon will illuminate the sea / Life is beautiful / The sun, yellow road / And the waves, the waves, the waves, the waves // Wobble / Stumble / It's a hard fall / Hard to come to one's senses / She left her family / Drank poison / And she's going to die of laughter // Wander / Daydream / She's been beaten a lot / But for those who know how to see / The flower is also / An open wound / And you can't see her crying / The sun will shine on her road / The moon will illuminate the sea / Life is beautiful / The sun, yellow road / And the waves, the waves, the waves, the waves.

"Dura na Queda" would become the opening song for Elza Soares' next groundbreaking album, *Do Cóccix Até o Pescoço*. Released in 2002, the album's musical director was José Miguel

Wisnik. In addition to being an excellent composer, Wisnik is known as one of the great writers and thinkers on the subject of Brazilian music. The record marks a turning point in Elza's career, combining her versatility as a performer with first-rate production value. At the time, Wisnik explained how the concept for the album was born [2022]:

> *I saw her show at SESC Pompéia in São Paulo in 1997, and my jaw dropped. Of course I knew Elza as a great singer, but I saw that she was so much more than I had thought. I perceived her ability to move through various genres, to create fusions; her sense of improvisation, the swing, the emotional density. This had to be shown off. I went to do a show and invited her to participate. She sang my songs, and so there was a certain understanding, and a desire to make a record together. The role of the production team is to accommodate the artist's greatness. That's why she sings songs from various genres, some danceable and others emotional, whether old or very recent – so that she's not treated like a samba museum, but as a contemporary singer.*

Do Cóccix Até o Pescoço truly presents Elza in a range of styles, with a freedom she had only reached previously on the album *Somos Todos Iguais*. This time, however, the overall quality of the album was different. From the compositions and the production to the sophisticated and memorable performance by the singer,

Do Cóccix Até o Pescoço is a courageous and impeccable work of art. The record presents various facets of Elza, moving from a song about jealousy in the case of "Dor de Cotovelo" by Caetano Veloso *"O ciúme dói do leito à margem / Dói pra fora na paisagem / Arde ao sol do fim do dia / Corre pelas veias na ramagem / Atravessa a voz e a melodia"* ("Jealousy hurts from the riverbed to the banks / It hurts out in the landscape / It burns in the late-day sun / It runs through the veins of the foliage / It creeps across the voice and the melody") to the political protest song "Haiti" (by Caetano and Gilberto Gil), which is performed as a rap punctuated by the pandeiro of the virtuoso percussionist Marcos Suzano. Meanwhile, the song "A Carne" by Seu Jorge, Marcelo Yuka, and Ulisses Cappelletti (previously recorded by the group Farofa Carioca) in Elza's hands becomes another touchstone for her repertoire, with the refrain *"A carne mais barata do mercado é a carne negra"* ("The cheapest meat on the market is Black meat.")

Elza would never be the same again. Nearly 70 years old at the time, Elza fully embraced the artistic freedom she had achieved. She continued to reinvent herself in record after record, experimenting with new partnerships and new musical forms. If her new directions frightened the most puritanical of listeners, they quickly won over supporters among the youth, positioning her as one of the most important references for the younger generations. And her artistic provocations only increased with time.

In 2004, Elza released a new album, *Vivo Feliz*. Although she had already experimented with different electronically-based

styles in the past – such as funk carioca, rap, and electronic beats – this was her first record of electronic music, with styles ranging from drum and bass to Jamaican dub. The repertoire includes classics such as "Volta Por Cima" by Paulo Vanzolini and "Opinião" by Zé Kéti, as well as contemporary songs such as Fred 04's "Computadores Fazem Arte," the musical manifesto of the Recife-based Mangue Beat movement.

Vivo Feliz was produced by Arthur Joly, a member of the Brazilian electronic music group Mugomango. The album includes a range of featured artists, from Simone Soul of Funk Como Le Gusta, to the French rapper Pyroman, to guitarist Zé Paulo Becker. Becker plays on the beautiful recording of "Lata D'Água," Elza's own brilliant composition, which closes the album:

O samba me mandou dizer / Que precisa de tempo pra pensar / Ou mudar a cadência do samba do morro / Ou resolverá mudar o morro de lugar // Lata d'água na cabeça / É o estandarte que representa minha arte / Jogo de cena é a fome / Negra sempre foi o meu nome / Mas digo isso porque / Tenho o samba pra me defender / E o carnaval / Ciência e filosofia / Que domina o mundo inteiro / Simplesmente em três dias

The samba told me to say / That it needs time to think / Either change the cadence of the samba from the hillside shantytown / Or it will move the hillside away // The water bucket on my head / Is the banner that represents my art / Hunger is my mise-en-scene / Negra [Black Woman] was always my name / But I can say that because / I have samba to defend me / And Carnival / Science and philosophy / Which rule the whole world / With simplicity for three days

In the album's liner notes, Elza reintroduces herself to the audience, saying: "I'm not afraid to throw myself into the wind, even though I know I don't have wings to fly. If this is being crazy... Call me crazy!"

Following *Vivo Feliz*, Elza would spend eleven years without recording any new studio albums. In the meantime, she performed. She revisited her older repertoire in the beautiful live DVD *Beba-me* in celebration of her 70th birthday, and in 2009 she released the live album *Arrepios* with guitarist and friend João de Aquino, who had collaborated with her in 1980 on the album *Elza Negra, Negra Elza*. In *Arrepios*, Elza presented new versions of samba songs featuring Aquino's Afro-accented guitar.

Between 2012 and 2014, Elza underwent a series of surgeries to address spinal problems that resulted from her 1999 fall off stage. "At the time I didn't care, but then it got worse," she lamented. She began to perform sitting down, but this didn't stop her from maintaining the energy and joy of being on stage, nor the ability to surprise her audience. In 2015 she resumed making studio recordings with the release of an album of previously unpublished songs, *A Mulher do Fim do Mundo* (The Woman at the End of the World). The album featured an entirely different sound, influenced by the "dirty" or noise samba of a new generation of musicians and composers from São Paulo.

Elza confessed that she didn't know any of those musicians who moved in groups and collectives like Passo Torto, Metá Metá, and Clube da Encruza prior to starting production for *A Mulher do Fim do Mundo*. But the affinity was immediate. The idea for the album was born following Elza's participation in a show by songwriter and academic Cacá Machado. But from the beginning, the idea was to bring together a series of musicians from the younger generations to record samba classics in new guises.

As the project progressed, they decided to make a record only with original songs, created specially for Elza by songwriters from the new generation. More than 50 songs were submitted, from which the eleven that make up the album were selected. The repertoire selection process was intimate and relaxed: "The staff came here to my home, we sat on the floor, and we chose the songs," Elza explained.

With production by Guilherme Kastrup, artistic direction by Rómulo Fróes, and the participation of musicians such as Rodrigo Campos (cavaquinho, electric guitar), Kiko Dinucci (acoustic and electric guitar), and Marcelo Cabral (synthesizer), the album title was inspired by a beautiful poem written in 1941 by Murilo Mendes, a modernist author with a strong surrealist influence:

Metade pássaro

A mulher do fim do mundo
Dá de comer às roseiras,
Dá de beber às estátuas,
Dá de sonhar aos poetas.

A mulher do fim do mundo
Chama a luz com assobio,
Faz a virgem virar pedra,
Cura a tempestade,
Desvia o curso dos sonhos,
Escreve cartas aos rios,
Me puxa do sono eterno
Para os seus braços que cantam.

Half bird

The woman at the end of the world
Gives the rose bushes food,
Gives the statues drink,
Gives the poets dreams.

The woman at the end of the world
Calls the light with a whistle,
Turns the virgin to stone,

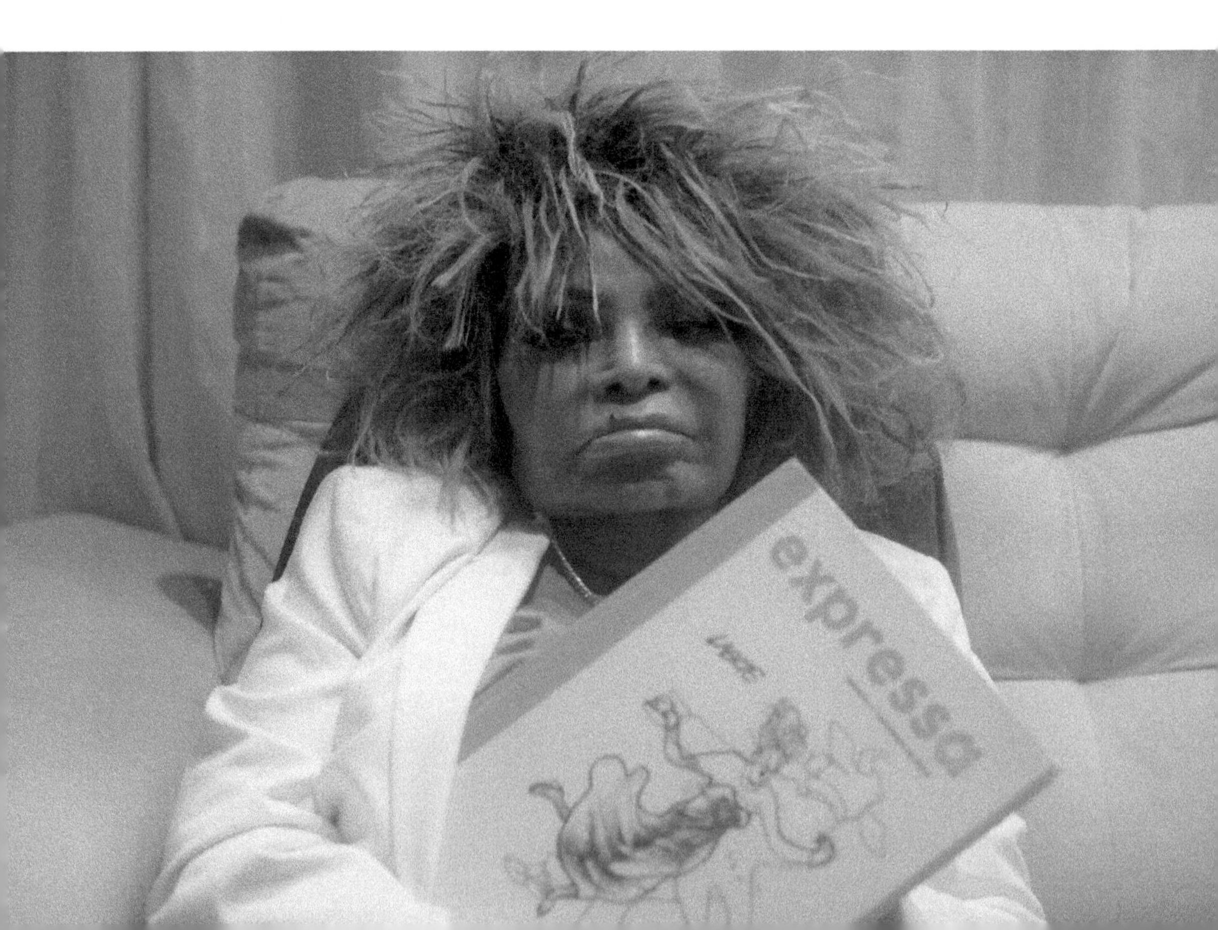

expresso

Heals the storm,
Diverts the course of dreams,
Writes letters to rivers,
Pulls me from eternal sleep
Into her singing arms.

The album begins with Elza singing unaccompanied on "Coração do Mar," a poem by Oswald de Andrade set to music by José Miguel Wisnik. The opening is followed by the title track, "A Mulher do Fim do Mundo," composed by Alice Coutinho and Romulo Fróes. The song ends with an intensifying and cathartic instrumental section, over which Elza declares: *"Mulher do fim do mundo / Eu sou, eu vou até o fim cantar / Mulher do fim do mundo / Eu quero cantar até o fim / Me deixem cantar até o fim"* ("Woman at the end of the world / That's me, I will sing until the end / Woman at the end of the world / I want to sing until the end / Let me sing until the end.") The "dirty" instrumental section, together with the singer's raspy voice, is emblematic of what Celso Sim aptly calls the album's "samba-punk" aesthetic.

Whereas Elza had previously presented herself as a "contemporary singer" in *Do Cóccix Até o Pescoço*, in *A Mulher do Fim do Mundo* she moved to the vanguard. The latter album has become a point of reference for popular musical experimentation in Brazil. Both albums also have strong political overtones, as for example in the song "Maria da Vila Matilde" (by Douglas Germano), which talks about violence against women; "Benedita" (by Celso Sim), a song about a Black transgender crack user; among others. The representations are raw, but without stereotyping or stigmatizing their protagonists.

As a whole, *A Mulher do Fim do Mundo* presents a far-from-rosy view of Brazil, foreshadowing the political climate that would come to dominate the late 2010s, a climate marked by growing authoritarianism, obscurantism, and poverty. This pessimistic perspective is made explicit in the lyrics of "Luz Vermelha," a song that references filmmaker Rogério Sganzerla and the famous phrase from his film *O Bandido da Luz Vermelha* (1968), "The Third World will explode, and anyone with shoes on will not be left":

> *"Telhado agora é porão tira de cima de mim esse pedaço de pedra / Me dá um abraço que o chão se abriu debaixo de nós e até o coxo tropeça / Bem que o palhaço falou que o laço vai se fechar e o laço sempre se fecha / Bem que o anão me contou que o mundo vai terminar num poço cheio de merda / Quem tinha tudo na mão quem não prestou atenção quem tem tamanco não sobra".*

> *The roof is now a basement, take this slab of stone off me / Embrace me, as the ground opens up beneath us and even the cripple stumbles / The clown did say that the noose will tighten and the noose always tightens / The dwarf did tell me that the world will end in a pit full of shit / Those who had*

everything, those who weren't paying attention, those who have heels on, will not be left.

A Mulher do Fim do Mundo received immediate critical acclaim, not only in Brazil but also on the international circuit. The album received rave reviews in the *New York Times* and in *Pitchfork* magazine, which considered the album one of the best of 2015. The album also won the Latin Grammy for Best MPB album the following year, and with good reason. It documents Elza at her best, not only as a performer, but also in her struggle against inequality of all sorts. As the tireless Elza herself said, "I was never afraid to stand up for what I believe. Because that's what being a woman is all about: defending what you think. I think the woman at the end of the world is the woman who still has her soul."

The partnership between Elza and the musicians who worked on *A Mulher do Fim do Mundo* would continue into the next album, *Deus é Mulher* (God is a Woman), from 2018. It was produced by Guilherme Kastrup, in partnership with Romulo Fróes, Kiko Dinucci, Marcelo Cabral, and Rodrigo Campos, and it featured more of a rock sound than the previous album. In the meantime, Elza was elevated into an icon of feminism, a subject which has gained more of a foothold in the Brazilian public sphere in the last several years.

The album *Deus é Mulher* begins with the beautiful song "O Que Se Cala" (That Which Is Silent), by Douglas Germano: "*Mil nações moldaram minha cara / Minha voz uso pra dizer o que se cala / Ser feliz no vão, no triz, é força que me embala / O meu país é meu lugar de fala*" ("A thousand nations have shaped my face / My voice, I use it to say that which is silent / Being happy in the abyss, on the edge, is the strength that cradles me / My country is my place of speech.") Voice is perhaps the album's main theme, appearing again in "Língua Solta" by Romulo Fróes and Alice Coutinho: "*Nós não temos o mesmo sonho e opinião / Nosso eco se mistura na canção / Quero voz e quero o mesmo ar / Quero mesmo é incomodar / Tem a voz que diz que não, não pode ser / Mas eu digo sim, que sim pro que eu quiser*" ("We don't have the same dream and opinion / Our echo mixes in the song / I want voice and I want the same air / What I really want is to be a bother / There's a voice that says no, you can't / But I say yes, yes to whatever I want.")

Elza's previous album had already expressed concern about the apparent failure of the national project of redemocratization. But by 2018, with the rise of the far right and the growing risk of losing civil rights, this expression of concern was becoming "a scream." As Elza said: "The time is ripe for the scream, of course. That scream cannot be silenced, it has to keep screaming, a lot.

6. Exu is an orixá of African cosmology with Yoruba roots, popularized in Brazil in African matrix religions such as Umbanda and Candomblé. Exu is the trickster, "the all-seeing one", "the one who is everywhere" and the beginning of all movement.

7. *Credo*, besides corresponding to a Christian prayer that begins with the Latin word credo (belief), it is also in Portuguese an interjection that expresses repulsion, displeasure, and could be translated as "God forbid").

Truly scream, without interruption." Social issues are clearly articulated on the album *Deus é Mulher*, with a political posture infused with defiance. The album is a wide-ranging affirmation of political values, including feminist ones like the right to eroticism and liberated sexuality (for example, "Eu Quero Comer Você," (I Want to Do You) which echoes the song "Pra Fuder" (Fucking) from the previous album) as well as secular values of religious freedom, as in "Exu nas Escolas"[6] (Exu in the Schools) as well as in the powerful song "Credo"[7] – "*Credo, credo, sai pra lá com essa doutrinação / Credo, credo, eu não quero medo me dando sermão.*" ("Credo, Credo, get lost with this indoctrination / Credo, Credo, I don't want to be afraid, giving me a sermon"). In fact, the album represents a continuation of the critical sensibility that accompanied Elza's entire career [2018b]:

> *I've been talking about politics since I started singing. About being a woman, about being Black. About being a Black woman. Domestic violence – no matter how much you discuss it and try to fight it – it's still very present. It's sad that you still have to make songs about violence against women, which is a horrible thing. Are we going to have to talk about it forever? It's a cancer, right? We talk about Blackness, we have to talk about skin color, which is absurd, right, to have to be constantly screaming, "look!", "look!" But over time, we see that it's important to talk and to keep talking. We hear the echo now, but the scream started a long time ago.*

These concerns are not only present in Elza's songs, but also in her public positions more generally. An example of this was the singer's 2018 intervention during an event at the Memorial da América Latina [2018]:

> *I received a tribute at the Memorial da América Latina in São Paulo, with a wonderful symphony orchestra, the Jazz Sinfônica. Great conductor, great musicians, a beautiful tribute. The moment I saw the symphony though, I felt strange. I didn't see one Black person in that symphony. So I asked, where are my Black people? What are they doing? Please, fight for this, seek it out, because you too have this right. Really, we have the right. And when I sang "the cheapest meat on the market is Black meat" I was praised when I said I felt the absence of Black people in that orchestra.*

But it's not just in relation to feminist and Black struggles that Elza has become an icon. The LGBTQIA+ audience, which was always present in her life, also embraced her again, in recognition of decades worth of love and attention [1997b]:

> *I'll tell you something: every woman is a bit of a man. We're all a bit gay. The woman is a natural leader, she's the*

8. A derogatory term for a gay man that has been reclaimed by some sectors of the LGBTQ community in Brazil.

*one who's always in front of the man. But society is still very
conservative, and women end up oppressing themselves. I'm
often judged because I do what I want, when I want. Otherwise,
I wouldn't be who I am today. That's where happiness is. And I
have great affection for gay people. When I lost my son, it was
the gay world who came to my rescue. They always call me
and encourage me: "Where's the new record, veado?"[6] That's
what they call me. And I really am gay! Just look at the way I
am. The only thing is that I like men.*

It was therefore no coincidence that the visual artist Laerte
Coutinho was invited to do the cover for Elza's next album, *Planeta
Fome* (2019). Laerte had also become a symbol of the LGBTQIA+
struggle, after coming out as transgender in 2010. This album
contains echoes of Elza's previous ones while including some
significant changes. The producer, Rafael Ramos, is more associated with rock than with experimental music, and has worked
with artists like Los Hermanos, Pitty, and Cachorro Grande. The
connection with rock is clear in the sound of the album, which is
a bit easier on the listener. In additon, the lyrics are less hopeless
in tone, although they maintain an element of social protest.

Planeta Fome opens with "Libertação" (Liberation), composed
by Russo Passapusso and recorded with BaianaSystem and Virgínia
Rodrigues. The compelling groove laid down by the Bahian band
is the backdrop for lyrics with strong political undertones. The
lyrics recall the refrain "ninguém solta a mão de ninguém" ("No

one lets go of anyone's hand") that circulated on social media in the face of escalating right-wing political extremism in Brazil: "*Eu não vou sucumbir / Eu não vou sucumbir / Avisa na hora que tremer o chão / Amiga é agora, segura a minha mão*" ("I won't succumb / I won't succumb / Let me know when the ground shakes / Girlfriend, the time is now, hold my hand.")

As the album title indicates, *Planeta Fome* looks back across Elza's entire artistic trajectory. The most poignant reference is to Elza's earlier hit "A Carne," performed here by rapper Rafael Mike in the song "Não Está Mais de Graça": "*A carne mais barata do mercado não 'tá mais de graça / O que não valia nada agora vale uma tonelada*" ("The cheapest meat on the market is no longer free / What was worthless is now worth a ton.") Although *Planeta Fome* doesn't have the same experimental potency as the previous albums, it reveals Elza the artist in her full vitality, giving voice to contemporary themes and "bothering" the status quo like only she can do. The album also represents the consolidation of a kind of freedom for which Elza fought over so many years – the freedom to have full control over what she says and sings [2018]:

> *I always had a very unique musical language. But when you're a poor Black girl who walks into a record company wanting to sing, you have to obey. Either you sing what you're given to sing, or you're not employed. And I needed to be someone because of my voice. Once I could stop obeying, I did. I showed*

what was inside me. I freed myself to sing what the youth likes, what I like, to sing new things. Singing with these kids is great. It's about the love of doing it.

Right up until her death on January 20, 2022, Elza remained desirous and desired, inspired and inspirational, with all the strength of an individual who, despite all the difficulties, knew how to make a living making art.

BIBLIOGRAPHICAL REFERENCES:

1962. *Cruzeiro* magazine. Rio de Janeiro, May 1962.

1963. *Intervalo* magazine, Rio de Janeiro, 16 February 1963.

1985. Bôscoli, Ronaldo. "A volta por cima de Elza Soares". *Manchete* magazine, April 1985.

1997. Louzeiro, José. *Elza Soares: Cantando para não enlouquecer.* Globo, Rio de Janeiro.

1997b. "Sou gay, mas gosto de homem". Interview with Elza Soares. *Istoé* magazine, São Paulo, 24 September 1997.

2002. "Flor Vertical". Interview with José Miguel Wisnik. *Folha de São Paulo* newspaper, July 2, 2002.

2008. Lichote, Leonardo. "Beba-me". Interview with Elza Soares, *Jornal O Globo* newspaper.

2016. Souza, Tárik de. *MPBambas - história e memórias da canção brasileira.* Kuarup, Rio de Janeiro.

2016b. Souza, Tárik de. *Sambalanço, a Bossa que Dança.* Kuarup, Rio de Janeiro.

2018. Camargo, Zeca. *Elza.* Leya, São Paulo.

2018b. Lichote, Leonardo. "*Deus é Mulher* tem presença feminina maior que no disco anterior". Interview with Elza Soares. *O Globo*, Rio de Janeiro, March 14, 2018.

2019. Post on Elza Soares' Facebook. September 2, 2019.

"I MISS TOMORROW"

An interview with Elza Soares, conducted by Ana Paula Simonaci, Leonardo Lichote, Paulo Almeida and Sergio Cohn in October 2019

Elza, your most recent album is called Planeta Fome, _which is, in a way, a return to origins, to the place of your childhood. That place is always present in your music. What was this environment like?_

It's funny, with everything I do, I go back. Did you know there are times when I see myself carrying water, like I used to do as a child? That never died. It was so alive, it was so strong in my memory, in my head, that it doesn't go away. Sometimes I still find myself thinking about the water bucket when I'm talking to people. And I say: "How crazy is that!" It's so I don't forget the past. I always recall that place, that time, so I don't forget that _fome_ and _fama_ [hunger and fame] are only two vowels apart. Hunger and fame. _Fome_ and _fama_. I can't forget where I came from.

I spent my childhood surrounded by misery. Dona Rosária, my mother, was a washerwoman. She washed rich people's clothes and I used to look at those beautiful dresses and linen sheets. I'd always find a way to put on a little dress or sleep on one of those bed sheets before my mother took them back to the ladies. There were six of us siblings. Only five were left. Malvina had died of hunger and pneumonia. We didn't have plates. We used to eat out of guava paste cans. My father would pound down the sides with a hammer so we didn't cut our hands. That was my plate. My cup was a can of condensed milk. Back then, we each had a mug like that. For drinking water or coffee, that was what we had. When things were tight, I went to the housing complex for military families to find scraps of food.

I lived through a lot and I suffered a lot too. Nobody gets used to suffering. But I learned to turn those moments into lessons. I carried a lot of water on my head and eventually I understood that this hideous bucket was a crown. A beautiful crown. Elza with the bucket of water on her head, who let her body get wet so she could show off her sensuality, right?

She was a sensual girl.

A really naughty girl. And it was by carrying that bucket of water that I learned my singing. I'd pick up the water and let out a groan, "grrroh!" And I thought, "This is going to be my sound!" My father was terrified by that. He'd say I was going to end up blowing out my throat. But I used to say, no, that was going to become music. And it did become music, and I started singing like that.

And with the praying mantis, right?

Yes! I'm in love with praying mantises. The praying mantis has a sound it makes, a "grrrrr," which, much later,

I started using in my singing. It was also thanks to the praying mantis that I got the inspiration to sing the way I sing. I used to take that little animal and put it close to my ear to listen. I loved that raspy noise. And I started making that little sound too.

You got married because of
a praying mantis, didn't you?

Yes. Because I was a tomboy. I used to live out in Água Santa[1] and I was a troublemaker. I only started wearing a skirt after I got married. I lived up in the trees in shorts and suspenders. I didn't even know what sex was. What I most wanted was to spin tops and fly kites. To play hopscotch. But my father, Avelino Gomes, was a very strict man. He was one of the founding members of the Partido Integralista.[2] He was a musician too. My father was a quarry worker, but he played the guitar. He was a trombonist, too. I have a photograph of my father with a trombone in his hand.

He worked every day at the quarry, and I would bring him coffee at 2 in the afternoon. With some fritters, all very greasy, all stuck together. Until one day I saw a beautiful praying mantis and I went into the undergrowth to catch it.

1. Neighborhood in the North Zone of Rio de Janeiro.
2. Partido Integralista (1932-1937), an ultra-nationalist, conservative, Catholic and extreme right-wing political and social movement, inspired by Italian fascism.

But an older boy saw me going into the woods and he went to see what I was doing. He scared the praying mantis, I tipped over the coffee pot, and I got so mad that I started fighting with the boy. It was a terrible fight, I wrestled with him in the woods, I got all bloody and everything. My father noticed I was late, he went to see why I wasn't there, and he caught me tangled up with the boy in the woods.

At that time, virginity was a very serious thing. My father thought the boy was trying to take advantage of me and he ordered us to get married. But I was still pure. So I got married at the age of 12, because of a praying mantis. But even so, I still love praying mantises...

How was your wedding?

The wedding was beautiful, with a veil, a bridal tiara, and everything else. But our relationship was very difficult. Back then, all I cared about was playing marbles and playing in the street. But the kid I married would go and break my kites, he'd ruin the wooden tops I liked so much. He'd destroy all my childhood games. And that's how I began adolescence. My husband only knew how to make children. He liked taking it easy. He worked at the quarry too, and he got tuberculosis, which made my life even more difficult. He left me a widow before I was 21 years old.

Yes. I needed to be able to support my children from an early age, so I worked. I went to work at the Veritas soap factory, in Engenho de Dentro.[3] My salary was pitiful, but I couldn't work overtime to get more money because I had no one to leave my son with, João Carlos. Then I went to work at the hospital kitchen in Engenho de Dentro. I was fired from the factory because I sang at lunchtime and people came to listen, which drove my boss crazy. I always sang. I think I was born singing. José Louzeiro wrote a book about me about 20 years ago called *Cantando Para Não Enlouquecer* ["Singing to Stay Sane"]. I was the one who came up with the title. It's something I've said many times, that singing for me is good medicine. If I didn't sing, I'd die.

I first started singing in public on Ary Barroso's TV show, "Calouros em Desfile" [New Talent On Parade]. I went there because I needed money to take care of my son, who had health problems. I had to convince Samuel Rosenberg, the man responsible for signing up the participants, to let me sing, because I was still very young. I had to explain that I really needed that money. But then, later, there was another problem. I was a very skinny teenager and I didn't have

3. Neighborhood in the North Zone of Rio de Janeiro.

clothes to perform in. So I took a skirt from my mother, which was huge on me. I fastened the clothes with some safety pins and put my hair in pigtails. The only way I had of hiding the extra cloth was using the pins. When I got on stage, everyone laughed. But I wasn't concerned about that, I just wanted to sing. It didn't matter that the audience made jokes about me or the way Ary Barroso asked, laughing: "What planet did you come from, my dear?" I replied: "From Planet Hunger, Mr. Ary."

Since then, safety pins have been a part of my life. They are always present. The outfit for the concert I did at the Rock in Rio festival was a jumpsuit held together with pins. The same reason: to remind me of where I came from.

**You won some money on
Ary Barroso's show, right?**

Yeah, a few bucks, which was enough to save my son. The prize money had built up, so it was good money for those days. But there was a problem, because the show was on Saturday and the prize was only paid on Wednesday, and I didn't know that. I needed the money that very night so I could go home. It was late at night, and I only had money for public transportation – but how was I going to walk up the hill into the slums in that outfit at night? So I had to take a taxi for the first time in my life. Without money.

Luckily, the driver agreed to let me pay later, once I picked up the prize money.

**And when did you have your first opportunity
to sing professionally?**

My brother was studying at a music school in Méier[4] with the teacher Joaquim Negli. I went because they needed a singer. I knew if I auditioned I might be selected. There I was, in the middle of all these girls, all of them rich, cute, white, and wonderful. Can you believe I got the spot? And the teacher even gave me a dress, because I didn't have clothes. He even had an outfit made for me to wear the night I had to sing with the Bailes Garan Orchestra. It was a filo dress, all white. I felt like a ballerina wearing that. The Orchestra held many events, and I always went with them. But sometimes I couldn't go on stage, because there was a club that was racist and didn't want a Black woman singing.

And what was the Orchestra's repertoire?

Ah, we played a lot of samba and samba-canção.[5]

4. A middle class neighborhood in the North Zone of Rio de Janeiro.
5. Samba-canção is a slower and more lyrical subgenre of samba that was highly influenced by bolero; popularized by Brazilian radio singers of the 1940s

Elza, do you dream a lot?

Boy, do I ever!

**And what are you like in your dreams? Are
you in the place you came from? Is it like it is
today? What do you dream about?**

It's funny, I never dream about today. You reminded me
of something good. I'm never in the present. I'm always
somewhere, but not today. I dream a lot about my family.
Things I experienced. Singing, talking. I talk a lot with the
son I lost, you know? Almost every night I dream about
Gilson, who died a few years ago. I talk to him a lot. He
brings bread for me to eat. My son is gone, but he is present
every night in my dreams.

How do you relate to this in spiritual terms?

I went through all the religions looking for protection. I
liked Buddhist philosophy, for example. But I'm a Catholic.
And every Catholic is a little bit Spiritist. Maybe I'm more
Spiritist than anything else. I believe we can't just be one
single thing, coming into the world and dying as if that were
everything there is. I believe that the spirit lives on. Think
about when you're talking to yourself: are you talking to

yourself or is someone speaking with you, helping out? I feel like there's something to that. It's all very strange.

And the singing?

The singing too. In my singing, there's a lot of Mr. Avelino, my father. I feel my father a lot, I have a deep affection for him. So in everything I do, I call on Mr. Avelino. After my father passed away, I came back from Argentina in bad shape. My career practically started in Buenos Aires. I went with Mercedes Baptista to Buenos Aires as a singer. She needed a Black singer with some body awareness and expressivity. So I got to know Buenos Aires before I even knew where Ipanema and Leblon[6] were. I remember Mercedes giving me one condition. She said: "My daughter, I took you out of there, if you don't behave yourself, I'll send you back on a cargo ship." But there was no need, because I became the ensemble's main attraction. I spent a year in Argentina, and I came back when my father died. And it was the right time, because my children, who stayed with my mother, were already missing me.

In Argentina, we had a great deal of trouble with the managers. Throughout my life, managers have always been a problem. When I came back, I dreamed that my father

6. Elite seaside neighborhoods in Rio de Janeiro with a thriving nightlife scene in the 1950s.

was telling me I was going to have a very good future singing. He asked me to sing "Ave Maria do Morro" for him. It's as if I can see it now: I was singing to my father, who was short of breath, and he got better and better. I sang "Ave Maria do Morro" and he said, "My daughter, don't be sad, you will have a life where you'll go through a lot of difficult things, but you will have a very good future." And there you go, what he said is happening. I saw Mr. Avelino.

**What was the experience
in Argentina like?**

When I started traveling the world to perform, I realized this was what I wanted to do. But the experience in Argentina was hard, with Mercedes Baptista it was cruel. She was also tricked by the manager. We had to stay there, and I sang to support the group. I sang at night at the Teatro Astral, [Astor] Piazzolla's nightclub, and in other clubs too, in order to earn money to support those who stayed. Mercedes Baptista left, but we stayed. Nobody had money to go back, understand?

We went through a lot of hardship, but it was also a very important experience in my life. I sang a lot in Argentina. I sang alongside Astor Piazzolla. I became very good friends with Piazzolla. He was very affectionate when I needed him in Buenos Aires. And playing in clubs was very important for me, because it taught me how to sing everything. I learned to be a "crooner" there. When you're a crooner, you have to know how to sing any style: samba, bolero, tango. You have to know how to sing everything. Waltz, mambo, cha-cha-cha. I even learned to sing blues and jazz, which was very important when I substituted for Ella Fitzgerald, years later, in Italy.

In Argentina, I was very young. I discovered another world there. I saw people who didn't eat from a can, but with a plate, a fork, and a knife. Actually I already knew that existed, because my mother, when she was going to deliver the clothes she washed, the ladies would ask her if she had already eaten, and she would say yes, but I'd say no. And they would serve us. The food came on a plate, with a fork and a knife. My mother taught us that we had to leave a little bit of food on the side of the plate. We had to leave a piece of meat – which we never got to eat at home – in the corner of the plate because it was polite to leave some food. The tastiest part, we had to leave it. And this is how I was raised. This is Elza.

**What's the story of you sitting
in for Ella Fitzgerald?**

Ella needed someone to replace her because she was having cataract surgery. She was doing "Ella Canta Tom

Jobim" [Ella Sings Tom Jobim]. So Naná Vasconcelos recommended me. At the time, I was living in Italy. So we had a big dinner, with a beautiful spread. Me, Ella, Jorge Ben, Trio Mocotó, and Mané. An unforgettable night. Luck was on my side. Elza and Ella, what a pair!

I met Oscar Peterson, too. I sat practically right next to him. He was lovestruck, because he had seen me singing at the theater and said, "What a voice!" I didn't understand anything he was talking about. But there was Frank, who was the manager, and he translated. Oscar Peterson was very impressed with me, because I was skinny, and even though I was skinny, tiny, petite, I brought the house down!

There's a live album of you and Jorge Benjor in Italy...

Man, I love Ben! Jorge Ben's arrival in Rome was awesome. But he's really afraid of thunderstorms. Jorge Ben is afraid of thunderstorms, ok people? If it thunders, don't wait for him, because he won't come.

What are you afraid of, Elza?

Of fear. I'm afraid of fear. If fear comes, I don't know what to do with it. So far, I've faced everything. I think I'm afraid of fear.

***What have you always
liked to listen to, Elza?***

Once I learned what was what, I started listening to
Chet Baker. To this day, that's my passion.

Why? What do you see in his music?

Man, I think he cries the music on his trumpet. Such
pain! That does me good. I love Chet Baker. I'm in love
with his music. When I started following Chet Baker and
his story, I was even a little angry with Miles Davis, because
of their fight, right? I like Miles Davis too, but Chet Baker
affects me in an amazing way.

***You were a crooner here in
Rio de Janeiro too, right?***

Yes. I was really lucky to work as a crooner in a nightclub, not only in Argentina, but here in Rio too. The Texas
Bar nightclub, in Leme, was really a school for me. It was
Moreira da Silva who took me there to sing. I was doing
all the auditions I could to be able to sing for a living. If
there was an audition, I was going to do it. And at one
of them, I met Moreira da Silva. I'd been on TV Tupi for
the Sunday program with Maestro Cipó. And Moreira da

Silva was delighted with the hoarseness of my voice and asked me: "My daughter, you're not interested in singing at night, are you?" I asked him what singing at night meant, and he said in a nightclub. And I said: "I don't even know what a nightclub is..." But I accepted and he introduced me to Aérton Perlingeiro, who ran the Texas Bar. I went and auditioned, I was selected, and I started singing at the club. And I earned good money for someone who'd never earned anything: 8 thousand cruzeiros...

**And what was this environment like?
Was there a lot of harassment?**

There was a lot. I suffered a lot of harassment, my goodness! It's just that I didn't place much importance on it. I was widowed very young, I had my children, and I was also very scared for my mother, you know, who took care of the children. But it turned out fine. I went there to sing and not to be catcalled, thank you very much!

Did you have fun on stage?

I have so much fun, to this day! Every time I get on stage, I feel great. I was born for the stage. Without the stage I'm nothing, I'm someone else, I'm Elza Gomes da Conceição, not Elza Soares. When I walk on stage, I feel wonderful. I feel like the hottest Black woman, like the most seductive woman!

What were the musicians like who accompanied you in those days?

In those days, there were very good musicians. Like today, by the way. And I was fortunate to play with some of the best. I remember Lúcio Alves, João Gilberto. Lúcio Alves was the king of improvisation, of vocalizing in the middle of the song. He was wonderful. And João was a really great friend. He used to go home, sit with his guitar, and sing. He was married to Astrud and she would tell me to let her know when he got in. But João would ask me to say he wasn't there. Then she would call, and I would say: "He's not here, okay, honey?" And by the "okay" she already understood that he was there.

João Gilberto was a great friend. I miss João very much. I watched him very young too, when he was a kid. He was there during my time at Odeon. Him, Lúcio Alves, a nice bunch. Ronaldo Bôscoli once wrote that I had an affair with João. Lies! He was my best friend and if I went out with him, I'd have been betraying not only Astrud, but also Milton Banana. I had an affair with Milton, yes. Milton was awesome. I was very lucky with the Miltons in my life:

Milton Banana, Milton Miranda, Miltinho. Miltinho, with whom I formed a duo, was wonderful. He had rhythm in the tips of his hair even... Back then, I spent time with all these fantastic musicians, many of whom were starting bossa nova. And of course, they were trying to seduce me. Tom Jobim, for example, was in love with me. But I pretended I didn't understand. What I really wanted was to bring milk home to the children.

You met Lupicínio Rodrigues
at the club, didn't you?

See, the problem is, I used to get anxious about singing at night, because I didn't really know how to deal with that universe of the club, with the harassment and all that. So I made some mis-steps. Lupicínio was one of them. I was singing in the club, and I saw a man sitting all in white, with a bouquet of roses. He kept looking at me. And I got nervous, because I thought he was another one who was going to harass me. And then, when the performance was over, he came over and said, "Pardon me, roses for a rose." And I scowled at him and said, "My name isn't Rose, and I don't like roses!" And he replied, "I know your name is Elza. My name is Lupicínio Rodrigues and I'm the author of 'Se Acaso Você Chegasse,'" the song I'd just recorded that was becoming a hit. I was so embarrassed, I tried to salvage it, but there was no way. It was an unpleasant situation, but we ended up becoming good friends.

It wasn't my only mis-step at the club. Even before that story, I remember one night I was there, and a girl passed by dancing. I was already tired of being harassed by men and suddenly that woman came right up to me, dancing. I found it very strange! She invited me to sit at her table when I finished singing. I replied that I had been hired to sing, not to go to anyone's table. So she introduced herself, and said she was Sylvinha Telles! And she joked that I seemed like a wild animal, I was so standoffish. She was married to Aloysio de Oliveira, who was a music producer. Also at her table there was Lúcio Alves, Roberto Menescal, and a director for Odeon. That's how I joined Odeon. I was becoming a hit at the club, I had more and more regulars, and that got the label's attention. Fame is like a rumor: it runs wild.

I was very lucky to have met the successful singers of the time, who helped me a lot at that moment. I wore one of Sylvinha's red blouses on the cover of my first LP, the very same one with Lupicínio Rodrigues' song, "Se Acaso Você Chegasse." Ângela Maria also dressed me well, she gave me many dresses to sing in...

**What was your marriage
with Garrincha like?**

I met Garrincha because of a Simca Chambord, can you believe it? Garrincha went to my house to ask for my support as part of a contest they were doing. I think it was for the most popular soccer player in Rio. The winner would receive a Simca Chambord, which was a luxury car. I barely knew who he was, but he already knew about me. I was already Elza Soares, signed by Odeon. He went to my house with Nilton Santos to ask for my support in the contest.

He was worried, because it was a competitive field. He was competing against [national team captain Hilderaldo] Bellini, for example. I was supposed to sell raffle tickets, but since I didn't know how to do that, I decided to buy them all myself. We fell in love and we spent 17 years together. I was so in love with him. When he was sober, Garrincha was the most beautiful thing in the world. He was a kind child. But he drank every day. At the end, he'd drink until he dropped. It was sad.

And we were attacked a lot. There was a lot of meanness. They accused me of having stolen Garrincha from another woman, because he was married and already had seven children. We started getting repeated threats, by letter, by phone. They said they would kill us if we didn't leave the country. We started to think it wasn't just a prank call. Then they machine-gunned our house, and we decided to leave. I was practically kicked out of the country. I had to leave. I went to Italy with Mané, because I needed to leave. I had nowhere else to live. We went to Rome.

**In Rome, did you have
a lot of contact with
Chico Buarque, who was
also living there?**

Yes. Chico was my very good friend. I also have a real love for Chico Buarque. At the time, Chico and Marieta Severo were a couple. They were my good friends. And also Mané's. Mané found a great friend in Chico. If he hadn't had Chico, he wouldn't have been able to stand staying in Rome. Man, how are you gonna go for a walk with your birdcage in Rome, wearing your board shorts, carrying a bird cage? It doesn't work, right? Because that's what Mané's life was like here in Brazil. I thought he suffered a lot. And with Chico, the two of them would go out, and that was that. Chico didn't leave Mané by himself. He took good care of Mané. Chico is everything, isn't he?

My relationship with Mané was very difficult. The pain was really strong. The pain was even stronger at times... no! Love was much stronger, because love fought pain. If it wasn't for love, we wouldn't have stuck it out. There was a great love at the center of it all that contained the battle. Because the battle was fierce. What a battle! What a battle!

And at that time, I suffered a lot of attacks from women too. It's important to draw attention to this – at that point in time, women weren't friends with women. There wasn't friendship, because women were thought to be false. But that's changed. Today, the projects I do are about uplifting women and bringing women to me. Because we're seeing the need for female friendship.

*You nourished and were nourished
by this current moment of the
feminist movement, right?*

A lot. I was born a feminist, you know? Because I was always questioning, "God, why do you let me carry water? God, why do you let me be hungry? God, why did you hurt my mother's foot? God, why do we live in a wooden shack with a tin roof that makes so much noise when it rains?" I was always questioning. With every "why" in my life, I always called on God. That's why I say God is a woman, because in the end I discovered that God was always on my side. And with all this questioning, I ended up getting this far and achieving so much.

*Who were the main women
in your life?*

My mother. My mom was a major woman in my life. Today I have my granddaughter, Vanessa, who is a major woman in my life. But the main woman in my life was my mother, Dona Rosária.

How do you remember her?

Poor thing, a lot of suffering, right? My mother was a woman who suffered a lot. A bucket fell on my mother's leg and burst a varicose vein. It couldn't heal, because they said that if it healed, she would die. So she spent her whole life with that scar on her leg, washing clothes, so many clothes, carrying so much water… Dona Rosária was a saint.

***Did you think your life was
going to be that way too?***

No. "Mother, I don't want your life for myself." And she was afraid, right? "What do you mean you don't want this life? What life do you want for yourself?" I'd say, "A better life. I want a plate, a fork, bedsheets." The basic things. The stuff I didn't have, that was what I wanted. But the one thing I never wanted for myself ever again was hunger. Not for me, not for my kids. That's why I fought, man! I struggled. It wasn't easy.

*And is there hunger
in your singing?*

Hunger is there, in everything. Hunger is present. Today I say we're hungry for healthcare, respect, credibility. Brazil is so bankrupt. And I'm hungry for it, you know? Hungry for culture. These desperate youth – all this is hunger.

*What was your reaction when
you saw the musical* **Elza?**[8]

I was very emotional! I cried! Even I wondered how a person could go through all that and get to see her own story on stage. There I am, guys! That's me! I cried a lot. I went through so much in my life...the musical didn't show even half of it. Speaking of hunger... Talking about being hungry is normal, but being hungry is hard. I know hunger right away. It was my companion many times, that damn hunger. It was my partner, my friend, my sister. It was all of that. That's why "Planeta Fome" is still with me.

*When you returned to Brazil and separated
from Garrincha, you went through a very
difficult phase of ostracism. Was there a*

8. Premiered in 2018, directed by Duda Maia, with libretto by Vinícius Calderoni.

*moment where you thought you wouldn't be
able to carry on?*

No. I never thought that. I always think things will work out. Maybe the moment I was closest to thinking like that was just before recording "Língua" with Caetano Veloso. Caetano is another person I love. I was thinking about quitting singing and going to work at an orphanage. I had my son Garrinchinha, who was still very little. I needed to feed my son, and I wasn't earning anything with music. So I said: "I'm going to stop singing and I'm going to work as much as possible. At least then I'll have money for food. I can eat, my son can eat..." But they told me to seek out Caetano. And I did. I said: "I came to say goodbye to you, because I quit singing." And he responded, "You have not! The queen bee can't leave her hive." I said, "But I'm not a queen bee." And he said, "You are. You're the one who's not getting it. To this day, you still haven't grasped the important role you play. Go back home and I'll come for you!"

He asked what I'd been doing in São Paulo. I said I'd worked in a circus, I sang in lots of places just to survive. Then I left for Rio with my son. There was a show at Teatro João Caetano at the time, called *Seis e Meia*. It was by Albino Pinheiro, and he invited me to participate. When I got there, I saw lines and lines of people to see Elza. I had to do two sessions. So there I was, the phone rang, and it was Caetano telling me not to leave the theater, to wait for him, that he was coming to pick me up. I wondered why. He hadn't forgotten his promise, and he took me to record "Lingua" with him. It was a beautiful recording, it turned out really well. That's why I say that luck is always on my side. As my friend Wilson das Neves used to say: "Oh, Luck!"

And "Língua" is almost a rap, right?

It is. "I like to feel my tongue brush Luiz de Camões' tongue." So good, right? "Flower of Lacio Sambadrome Powdered-Latin Luso-America. This tongue, what does it want? What can it do?"

**You always had an open ear
and a keen eye for new music
that was emerging...**

Totally. In order to be a singer, an interpreter of other people's compositions, you can't allow yourself to be labeled. You have to sing everything. When you sing, don't you sing whatever comes to mind? I always thought like that. I'm not a soft drink that needs a label. Let's sing whatever comes. I've already recorded everything. My life is very crazy, guys. Very crazy.

*Elza, even though you've lived
abroad, you love Brazil, don't you?*

So much. I remember when Mané and I decided to return to Brazil. Man, there's no place more beautiful, more wonderful than Brazil! I've traveled around and I can say: there isn't.

*Now you live in Copacabana, facing
the sea. You could live anywhere
in the world, why did you choose
Copacabana?*

Because I love it! I love this place here. I'd been here many times when I used to perform at the Texas Bar Nightclub. That's when I got to know Copacabana and discovered it was beautiful. Those convertible cars, those fancy women. Everyone was very fancy. Copacabana used to be very bright. Today Copacabana is kind of sad, there's no longer that same joy I remember. But it's still Copacabana. I like it. I'm in love with it here!

*Are you against this thing of leaving
Brazil and going to live abroad?
Do you think it's wrong?*

Oh, very wrong. Because today Brazil needs us all. It needs to be held. I think abandoning Brazil now is a crime. Please, let's stay here! We are the children of this land, and our parents need our help. This Rio de Janeiro, it's been cast aside! The streets are falling apart. And nobody takes action, nobody does anything. I think they put sedatives in the drinking water. Everyone is asleep. Nobody wakes up for anything!

***You say that your voice was a weapon,
and a blessing, but you always took
care of it too...***

I take care of it. I don't smoke, I don't drink. I'm afraid to, because it's my gift, right? And it's my future, it's here, in my throat. My voice. So I can't spoil such a divine gift. I take care of my throat, leaving her at ease. I talk to her, calm her down. I go to the doctor to see how she's doing, to see if she's rose-colored, beautiful, wonderful. I don't punish her with cigarettes or alcohol, because I think that would be a crime. God gave me this gift. It's a gift I'm very fond of. I went to the doctor the other day, and he said my throat is so clean, so rosy, it's shocking. He said it's the throat of a woman in her early 20s.

Has it always been like that?

***Have you always been
this conscientious?***

Always. Because if it wasn't for my voice, what would I have? I didn't have a chance to go to good schools, I didn't have money for education. By the way, I even went to college! I went to college in Bangu.[9] But on the first day of school, it was a disappointment. The boys left the classroom to smoke, because they didn't like the teacher. That's what we see today: the teacher is no longer respected. It's a pity, there's such a lack of respect for teachers. If I've said anything worthwhile here today, I have to give credit to my teachers.

What college was it?

Law School. I went to study law because [the pioneering Afro-Brazilian actor] Grande Otelo thought I needed to become a lawyer to defend Black people. He said, "Look here, miss, you have to become a lawyer, because as a Black lawyer you'll be able to defend your brothers and sisters." And that wasn't what I wanted at all. If it's about defending my brothers and sisters, I already do that without being a

9. Neighborhood in the West Zone of Rio de Janeiro.

lawyer, through my voice. And now I'm a doctor. Doctor Honoris Causa! And I achieved it my own way. Fighting, struggling, believing. I got this far, and I hope to get a little further.

Is there anything left that you haven't done? Somewhere you want to go?

When you're alive, everything is left! You're alive, you want things. I'm very curious. I think there's still a lot to see. Many things have yet to arrive. Didn't the computer arrive, the cell phone? Didn't the future arrive? This future that has so spoiled the past... Other things will come and when they do, I want to be present, to say, "Hey, look at me here!"

And do you think about what will happen when you're no longer here?

Oh no. I don't waste my time. My name is now.

Vinicius de Moraes has that line: "My time is when."

"My time is when!" That's so good. We know there will come a time when we won't be here anymore. But why talk about it? The time will come, and then it will have arrived. But for the time being, no. So we go on doing things. My name is now. I am now. I already know the past so well that I want to be the now. And later this "now" will pass. I don't think or plan too much. If I sit still thinking about tomorrow, I'm going to become very yesterday. And I don't miss yesterday. I miss the tomorrow that I don't know. I'm very blessed. Things come to me. And something that's very beautiful is getting to watch time go by. Knowing that you are inside the present, living it. There are people who don't even notice the passage of time. But it's good to live and know you've lived a lot, that you've experienced many different things.

You've always surrounded yourself with younger people, haven't you?

I enjoy it. [My producer] Pedro Loureiro, for example. I fight with him to get him to shave his beard and show that cute boyish face of his. I like him without a beard. Because, as long as you have a boyish face, why put on an old man's face? There will come a time when you'll want to look like a boy but it won't be possible any more. The moment will have passed – the past that passed.

***And do you learn
from young people?***

I learn a lot. I don't teach anything. I just keep learning, with these beautiful, wonderful, healthy kids. The beard notwithstanding, right?

***In recent years, you've been
recording new albums like
A Mulher do Fim do Mundo
with songs by young composers.
How did these projects come about?***

See, *A Mulher do Fim do Mundo* emerged from a show by Cacá Machado. We started talking about making an Elza record, but without knowing what it would be like. The first idea was to make a record of traditional songs with modern arrangements, with this wonderful bunch of young musicians. But then Guilherme Kastrup had the idea of making a record with only new songs, composed specifically for the record. And it was beautiful! It was a hit among young people. So we continued making other records, such as *Deus é Mulher* and *Planeta Fome*.

Do you still compose?

Yes. But there are many compositions I invited Pedro to partner with me on. There are a lot, aren't there, Pedro?

[Pedro Loureiro] It's impressive. We always travel together, and there's an important detail which is that Elza doesn't drink or smoke. After we get to the hotel, her idea of fun is for us to go eat brie cheese with apricot jam, and to have a cup of coffee, or coffee with milk. And then she'll talk about things. She'll lie down on the bed and talk about things and I'll write it down in a notebook. But there are also notebooks she wrote herself. One day she said, "Oh! Sit here so we can talk." And she gave me two notebooks to read. I didn't know what it was. It moved me so much I felt ill.

Because I've always written a lot.

[Pedro Loureiro] You wouldn't believe the stuff that's in these notebooks. It has to be published! It's crazy. The ideas, the lyrics, the memories – it's amazing! The recipe for the omelet she used to make for Garrincha is written down alongside a song and a thought

about life. There's a lot of energy inside these notebooks. You see two, three decades of Elza inside these notebooks. Some very well-worn pages. So I said, "Wait, I can't, I'm not strong enough!" and I closed it.

With this latest album, there's a very beautiful story that involves a new composer, Rafael Mike. He'd written a song that started, "The cheapest meat on the market is now free." And it was based on that song by Marcelo Yuka and Seu Jorge that I recorded in *Do Cóccix Até o Pescoço*, "The cheapest meat on the market is Black meat." And so I asked to speak to him, and I said: "Hey, it's not like that: the cheapest meat isn't free anymore." And the song went on: "What used to be worth a kilo is now worth a ton." I changed it to "what used to be worthless is now worth a ton." Because that's how it is: what was worthless is now valuable!

Me myself, who for a while was worthless, today I'm worth a ton. When I was sidelined, unable to perform, I was aware I wasn't worth anything for some reason, and I went in search of something to make me valuable. So I asked for the composer's permission to play with the lyrics a little. And Mike's story is very powerful for me. His father was my drummer. And he didn't know that. He was adopted at the age of two. They gave Mike to an Italian family. And he grew up wanting to know who his real parents were. He didn't have any information about them.

He started looking for his parents, and he managed to find his mother, who lives in Foz do Iguaçu. So he wanted to know who his father was, but she said he'd already passed away. He got really sad because he wanted to meet his father. It was very difficult for him with his mother, because she was a stranger. He didn't even know what to call her. And then she told him that his father went by the name Batista, and that he'd been the drummer for Elza Soares. And he wanted to ask me about it but he didn't know how. So he came and asked me if I knew any Batistas. I said yes, that he had been my drummer. Then he smiled, and I thought the smile was identical to his father's. His mouth was identical.

I don't know if it's fate, but there is something spiritual to it. Very powerful. Batista's son ends up being a composer for Elza Soares, recording on my album. That's really something, right? It's a fantastic story.

What was your biggest night on stage? Is there one that stands out?

Look, every night I go on stage, for me it's a special night. I say, "This night is mine." So I think it's every night.

I go out with a lot of enthusiasm, eagerness, and willingness to perform, so every night turns into "the" night. I'm looking forward to this new project now and to doing shows…

*You've always been a perfectionist
with the costumes in your shows,
haven't you? I remember the
Do Cóccix Até o Pescoço show,
the open back and those giant heels…*

Six inch heels! I transformed into a huge woman. But when I took off the heels, what happened to that woman? Where is she?

*But that's what a stage is for, right?
This fantasy…*

The stage is for growing. I grow on stage. Even today, I still grow on stage, even after having operated on my spine twice. I had upper and lower back surgery. I had pins put in because of the fall I took off the stage at the Metropolitan theater in 1999. It was quite a fall, more than six feet. But I fell, got up, dusted myself off, and here I am…

Are you in a lot of pain, Elza?

Sometimes I feel it. But I can deal with pain. I'm okay, I can take it. I can take my pain. I'm resilient.

José Miguel Wisnik once said about you, "Elza doesn't do drama. Zé Celso always says that drama is a bourgeois thing, and that tragedy is universal. Tragedy and carnival are born from the same source, from the rituals of Dionysus. And Elza drinks from that source."

José Miguel is a beautiful creature. I love his sensitivity, and his ability to be an intellectual who speaks the language of the people. When we worked together, he showed me that I could be more daring and play more with my voice. He was very important at that point in my career when I did *Do Cóccix Até o Pescoço*. By the way, do you know what we were going to call the record? *Foda-se*! [Fuck Yourself!] But then we decided to change the name, because nobody was going to go to the store and say: "I'm here to buy Elza Soares's 'Fuck Yourself.'"

Elza, you've recorded a lot of songs, do you have one that's your favorite?

"Meu Guri" was a really powerful one. Chico Buarque's song. I spent time enjoying this song in a way I can't even explain. I spent a lot of time singing and crying. I thought, "My God, I have to stop crying. Am I going to sing this song my whole life and still cry? I can't!" "Meu Guri" was one of those songs that hurt really good.

Why does this song make you think about your life?

Because you see Chico writing "Meu Guri" as if he was a kid from [the favela]. How did he manage to write "Meu Guri"? "When my little sprout was born, mister, it wasn't time for him to break out / He was born with a hungry face, I didn't even have a name to give him / I don't know how to explain how I carried on, I carried him to carry me / And in his childhood he told me once that he would get there / Look there, look there, look there, my boy." It's very powerful! Very powerful. This is Chico Buarque de Holanda, folks. People keep telling him "vai pra Cuba!" ("go to Cuba!")[10] But Chico, don't go to Cuba, my love. Stay here!

10. A common right-wing slogan in Brazil used to attack social critics perceived to be leftists or "Marxists".

He went to Paris temporarily,
right? To write a book...

He has an apartment there, right? We'd always meet on the street in Paris, when I lived there for a while. I used to run into him, "Hey, what are you doing here?" But Chico, I know things are very tough, but don't leave Brazil. If you leave Brazil, what will I do?

Does the political situation
in Brazil scare you?

It's a damn disease! I'm telling you, we've got a crazy flu on our hands. You have to be careful it doesn't turn into pneumonia, right? It comes on little by little. Did you see that book censorship thing at the Bienal?[11] But the response was beautiful. Right away people stood up and said "No!" The people have been silent, but when they open their mouths... We cannot let censorship and authoritarianism return. We have to fight, right?

Elza, in closing: when you look in the mirror,
how do you see yourself today?

11. In 2019, Rio de Janeiro's evangelical mayor attempted to have books depicting homosexuality removed from the Biennial Book Fair.

Look, to this day I don't see myself as a great artist, as a big star. I still see myself as a person, as a human being. This big-star thing scares me a lot. It really does scare me! You know, I think we're not great at all. We're ourselves, do you understand? When Ary Barroso said that a star was being born on stage, it scared me a lot. I started looking up to try to figure out what kind of star is born randomly like that. I like my simplicity, guys. I love my simple side.

But don't you like to see the greatness of this star? The one that touches and moves people?

Yes, but I can't stop being myself, in all my simplicity, to go live as this great star. Otherwise, how do I live?

Your newest record starts with the phrase "I will not succumb." You're a tough one, aren't you, Elza?

Yes! And I'm grateful for everything I've experienced! I had to experience sacrifice in order to reap the rewards – like my voice. "My voice, I use it to say what is silent." I always thought that my voice would be my livelihood, that it would be my life, that it would be my job. I always thought my voice would be everything. There is always a reward. And my legs. These legs – sculpted by so many years of climbing up and down the hill in the favela – I know that my legs – I always had good legs – they took me places. They took me to places where stuff was happening. But I can't explain it. I always ask myself why all this happened, but I still can't explain how I got here. I had everything against me: woman, Black, poor. Everything was against me. And it worked out.

TIMELINE

1937   Elza Gomes da Conceição is born on
June 23 in Rio de Janeiro.

1949   Elza's father, Avelino Gomes, forces
her to marry Alaúrdes Soares after an
incident involving a praying mantis.

1953   Elza first performs on Ary Barroso's radio program
"Calouros em Desfile" where she famously
quips that she "comes from Planeta Fome."

1958   Afro-Brazilian dancer-choreographer Mercedes
Baptista invites Elza to join the Balé Folclórico
Mercedes Baptista for a series of shows in Buenos
Aires, Argentina. Elza hones her craft as a "crooner"
in Buenos Aires' nightclubs, where she meets
the modern tango composer Astor Piazzolla.

1959   Elza records her first single for Odeon, featuring the
song "Se Acaso Você Chegasse" by Lupicínio Rodrigues.

1960   Elza records her first full LP for Odeon with
the same name, *Se Acaso Você Chegasse*.

1962   Elza travels to Chile to perform, where she becomes
"godmother" to the Brazilian national soccer
team during the 1962 World Cup, meeting Louis
Armstrong and falling in love with soccer star
Mané Garrincha (Manuel Francisco dos Santos).

1966   Elza and Garrincha are married.

1967   Elza releases the pioneering three-volume album *Elza, Miltinho e Samba* with percussionist and singer Miltinho.

1970   Elza and Garrincha leave Brazil to live in Italy following increasing threats and attacks. While in Italy, Elza is invited to substitute Ella Fitzgerald on her "Ella Canta Tom Jobim" tour.

1972   Elza releases the album *Sangue, Suor e Raça* on Odeon with pianist Dom Salvador and the relatively unknown artist Roberto Ribeiro. Elza fights with the label to give more opportunities to Afro-Brazilian artists.

1974   Elza leaves Odeon and makes her first of three recordings for Tapecar. Elza faces a series of personal and professional difficulties.

1977   Elza and Garrincha separate.

1979   Elza records two commercially unsuccessful albums for CBS.

1983   Garrincha dies. Elza decides to leave the artistic profession, but is convinced to record the song "Língua" for Caetano Veloso's album *Velô*, paving the way for her subsequent comeback.

1985   Elza records *Somos Todos Iguais* for Som Livre with special participation by Cazuza and other stars of the new Brazilian rock scene.

1986   Elza's youngest son dies in a car accident. Elza decides
to leave Brazil, residing for a time in Los Angeles.

1997   Elza returns to Brazil and records the album
Trajetória, with the special participation
of samba icon Zeca Pagodinho.

1999   BBC Radio London names Elza "Singer of the
Millenium." Elza suffers a spinal cord compression after
falling off the stage at the Metropolitan Theater in Rio.

2002   Elza releases the ambitious album *Do Cóccix
Até o Pescoço*, produced by composer and
intellectual José Wisnick, who seeks to showcase
her abilities as a "current and contemporary
singer" rather than a "samba museum."

2004   Elza releases *Vivo Feliz*, an album that
takes a deep dive into electronica.

2015   Elza releases the highly experimental album, *Mulher
do Fim do Mundo*, with all original compositions,
produced by Guilherme Kastrup; the album wins the
Latin Grammy for Best MPB Album the following year.

2018   Elza releases *Deus É Mulher*, further elevating
feminist issues in her music as the women's
movement takes center stage in Brazilian society.

2019   Elza releases her final album *Planeta Fome*, featuring cover design by LGBTQIA+ icon, Laerte Coutinho.

2022   January 20, Elza dies in Rio de Janeiro.

BIOGRAPHICAL REFERENCES

Aldir Blanc
(1946-2020). Lyricist, composer, and author who wrote more than 600 songs, many in collaboration with his main partner João Bosco. These include the classic "O Bêbado e a Equilibrista."

Alice Coutinho
(1985-). Lyricist and educator from Pernambuco state who collaborated with husband Rómulo Fróes on Elza Soares' album *Mullher do Fim do Mundo*.

Aloysio de Oliveira
(1914-1995). Songwriter, singer, radio announcer, and music producer from Rio de Janeiro. Artistic director for the record label Odeon who helped launch the international career of Carmen Miranda.

Ângela Maria
(1929-2018). Abelim Maria da Cunha. Singer and actress from Rio de Janeiro. Iconic figure of the samba-canção genre. Elected "Queen of Radio" in 1954 by the Brazilian Radio Association.

Antônio Maria
(1921-1964). Sports commentator, writer, and songwriter from Pernambuco. Composed the well-known "Manhã de Carnaval" with Luiz Bonfá.

Ary Barroso
(1903-1964). Songwriter and radio presenter from Minas Gerais who hosted Calouros em Desfile program for new talent. Among his compositions, "Aquarela do Brasil" stands out for having inaugurated the genre of "samba exaltação." Nominated for an Oscar for his song "Rio de Janeiro," composed for the 1944 film Brazil.

Astor Piazzolla
(1921-1992). Argentinian composer and bandoneon player, a central figure in the 20th century modernization and revitalization of tango.

Astor Silva
(1922-1968). Brazilian composer and tromboner player who performed samba, choro, and mambo, and conducted his own dance orchestra during the 1950s.

Astrud Gilberto
(1940-). Bossa nova singer from Bahia whose version of "Girl from Ipanema" is among the most famous bossa nova recordings of all time. Formerly married to bossa nova icon João Gilberto.

Ataulfo Alves
(1909-1969). Singer and songwriter of samba from Minas Gerais state. His songs were recorded by Carmen Miranda, Clara Nunes, Quarteto em Cy, among others.

Augusto de Campos
(1931-). Poet, essayist, and translator from São Paulo. Creator of Brazilian concrete poetry movement, along with Haroldo de Campos and Décio Pignatari. In 2015, he was awarded the Pablo Neruda Ibero-American Poetry Prize.

Beth Carvalho

(1946-2019). Singer and songwriter from Rio de Janeiro, a central figure in the samba and pagode genres, known as the "Godmother of Samba."

Cacá Machado

(1976-). Songwriter, academic, historian, and producer of Brazilian popular music.

Caetano Veloso

(1942-). Singer and songwriter from Bahia, one of the most influential Brazilian musicians of the 20th and 21st centuries. One of the prime movers of the Tropicalist movement of the late 1960s, and author of *Verdade Tropical* (1997), an important reflection on Brazilian popular music.

Cazuza

(1958-1990). Artistic name of Agenor de Miranda Araújo Neto. Singer and lyricist of 1980s Brazilian rock.

Chet Baker

(1927-1988). Singer and trumpet player from the United States, associated with cool jazz. Famous for his gentle singing voice which influenced Brazilian singers like João Gilberto.

Chico Buarque

(1944-). Singer and songwriter in the MPB genre whose songs are well-known for their lyricism and political critique. An award-winning novelist, winner of the Prêmio Camões in 2019.

Clara Nunes

(1942-1983). Singer and musical curator from Minas Gerais state, best known for her performances of folkloric, popular, and Afro-Brazilian music.

Cyro Monteiro

(1913-1973). Singer and songwriter from Rio de Janeiro. Best known as a singer of romantic samba-canção during the golden age of Brazilian radio in the 1930s, Monteiro also became associated with bossa nova later in his career.

Dalva de Oliveira

(1917-1972). Singer and composer from São Paulo. Central figure during the golden age of Brazilian radio. Named "Queen of Radio" in 1951. Recorded more than 400 songs and performed on several Carmen Miranda albums.

Dom Salvador

(1938-). Pianist, arranger, and songwriter, considered a central figure in samba jazz. During the 1970s, he founded the group Abolição, one of the most important and innovative groups to perform "Black Music" in Brazil.

Dorival Caymmi

(1914-2008). Singer and songwriter from Bahia whose songs focused on the culture and day-to-day life of his state. A major point of reference for the bossa nova movement, his major hits include "Saudade da Bahia," Samba da Minha Terra," "Doralice," and "Maracangalha."

Douglas Germano
(1968-). Composer, guitarist and singer from São Paulo, co-founder of Duo Moviola with Kiko Dinucci, known for his work in the experimental "samba torto" subgenre.

Duke Ellington
(1899-1974). Jazz composer, pianist, and bandleader, one of the most internationally well-known jazz icons of the 20th century.

Ed Lincoln
(1932-2012). Brazilian producer, songwriter, and multi-instrumentalist, known as the "King of Sambalanço."

Edu Lobo
(1943-). Songwriter, arranger and guitarist from Rio de Janeiro associated with the bossa nova movement, his songs include collaborations with Vinicius de Moraes and Chico Buarque.

Ella Fitzgerald
(1917-1996). U.S. jazz singer, famous for her virtuosic scat singing, and her ability to imitate instrumental timbres with her voice.

Francisco Alves
(1898-1952). Singer born in Rio de Janeiro. Considered one of the most important singers of the Golden Age of Brazilian radio; sang on the first recording of "Aquarela do Brasil."

Franco Fontana
(1934-). Italian music and theater producer.

Fred 04
(1962-). Fred Rodrigues Monteiro. Singer, musician, and songwriter from Pernambuco. Bandleader of Mundo Livre S/A, and one of the key members of the Mangue Beat movement in the early 1990s alongside Chico Science and Nação Zumbi.

Gonzaguinha
(1945-1991). Luiz Gonzaga do Nascimento Júnior. Singer and songwriter from Rio de Janeiro, son of Northeastern Brazilian icon Luiz Gonzaga. Gonzaguinha's songs were popularized in the voice of Gal Costa, Elis Regina, Maria Bethânia, among others.

Grande Otelo
(1915-1993). Sebastião Bernardes de Souza Prata. Actor, comedian, and songwriter from Minas Gerais. Major figure within Brazilian revue theater, and one of the first Black Brazilian screen actors.

Guilherme Kastrup
(1969-). Drummer, percussionist, and music producer from Rio de Janeiro, known for his eclectic style.

Guinga
(1950-). Carlos de Sousa Lemos Escobar. Composer and guitarist from Rio de Janeiro whose songs were recorded by

Elis Regina and Chico Buarque, among others.

Ismael Silva
(1905-1978). Singer and songwriter of sambas from Rio de Janeiro. One of the founding members of the first samba school in Brazil, Deixa Falar.

Jackson do Pandeiro
(1919-1982). José Gomes Filho (1919-1982). Singer and songwriter from Paraíba who combined rhythmic Northeastern genres, such as baião, xote, forró and coco, with samba.

João de Aquino
(1944-2022). Guitarist, producer, and songwriter who worked with some of the biggest names in samba and Brazilian popular music, including Candeia, Elza Soares, Carlos Cachaça, Leny Andrade, Monarco, Martinho da Vila, Roberto Ribeiro, Cartola and Elizeth Cardoso.

João Donato
(1934-). Pianist, accordionist, arranger, singer, and composer. His music is characterized by his use of jazz and Latin music, with a particular affinity for Afro-Cuban music.

João do Vale
(1934-1996). Singer and songwriter from Maranhão state whose songs include "Carcará," which was immortalized by singer Maria Bethânia.

João Gilberto
(1931-2019). Singer and guitarist from Bahia, one of the founding members of the bossa nova movement.

João Nogueira
(1941-2000). Singer and songwriter in the samba genre whose hits include "Espelho." Father of singer Diogo Nogueira.

Jorge Aragão
(1949-). Singer, songwriter, and multi-instrumentalist in the samba and pagode genres, known for hits such as "Enredo do Meu Samba."

Jorge Ben Jor
(1945-). Singer, songwriter, and guitarist from Rio de Janeiro. His album *Samba Esquema Novo* inaugurated a new style that later shaped the genres known as sambalanço and samba-rock. Considered one of the top 5 greatest Brazilian musicians by *Rolling Stone* magazine in 2008.

José Miguel Wisnik
(1948-). Musician, composer, academic, and historian. Known for his academic writing on Brazilian literature and popular music. Artistic director for Elza Soares' album *Do Coccix Até o Pescoço*.

Kiko Dinucci
(1977-). Music producer and guitarist from São Paulo, known for his eclectic and experimental approach to popular music.

Laércio de Freitas
(1941-). Songwriter, arranger, and pianist from Rio de Janeiro. Accompanied various MPB and samba musicians, including Maria Bethânia, Marcos Valle, Clara Nunes and Martinho da Vila.

Laerte Coutinho
(1951-). Cartoonist from São Paulo, recognized as an icon of the Brazilian LGBTQIA+ movement.

Lobão
(1957-). João Luiz Woerdenbag Filho. Singer and songwriter from Rio de Janeiro.

Louis Armstrong
(1901-1971). U.S. jazz singer and trumpet player, famous for his vocal timbre and his virtuosic scat singing.

Lúcio Alves
(1927-1993). Singer and songwriter born in Minas Gerais, based in Rio de Janeiro. One of the best-known radio performers of the early 1950s.

Luis Carlos Sá
(1945-). Singer and songwriter from Rio de Janeiro whose compositions were performed by Gal Costa, Elza Soares, Milton Nascimento, Erasmo Carlos, among others.

Lupicínio Rodrigues
(1914-1974). Singer and songwriter from Porto Alegre. Composed various carnival marches and samba-canção songs, in addition to the anthem for the Grêmio soccer club.

Mané Garrincha
(1933-1983). One of the most iconic names in Brazilian soccer. Played for Botafogo-RJ and the Brazilian national team, winning the World Cup in 1958 and 1962.

Marcelo Cabral
(1978-). Producer, composer, and bassist from Alagoas state. Active in various subgenres of Brazilian popular music, including samba and electronica.

Marcelo Yuka
(1965-2019). Songwriter, singer and political activist from Rio de Janeiro. One of the co-founders of the reggae-rock band O Rappa.

Marcos Valle
(1943-). Singer, composer, producer, and pianist from Rio de Janeiro associated with the genres of bossa nova and samba.

Marieta Severo
(1946-). Brazilian actor best known for her work in cinema, television, and theater. Formerly married to singer Chico Buarque.

Martinho da Vila
(1938-). Martinho José Ferreira. Rio de Janeiro based singer and songwriter of sambas, as well as an author. His best-known songs include "Batuque na

cozinha" (1972) and "Canta, canta, minha gente" (1974).

Mercedes Baptista

(1921-2014). Dancer and choreographer from Rio de Janeiro, considered pioneer of Afro-Brazilian dance and ballet in Brazil. First Black dancer to join the dance corps of the Teatro Municipal in Rio de Janeiro.

Miles Davis

(1926-1991). Trumpet-player and jazz icon from the United States, considered one of the central figures in the evolution of jazz fusion.

Milton Banana

(1935-1999). Antonio de Souza. Drummer from Rio de Janeiro who accompanied the central figures of bossa nova. Performed on the iconic João Gilberto album *Chega de saudade*.

Milton Miranda

(n.d.). Music producer and artistic director from Minas Gerais. Director of the record label Odeon, where he produced the albums of Elza Soares, Clara Nunes, Milton Nascimento, Paulinho da Viola, among others.

Moreira da Silva

(1902-2000). Singer and songwriter from Rio de Janeiro, also known as Kid Morengueira. Considered the creator of the "samba de breque" style.

Naná Vasconcelos

(1944-2016). Percussionist from Pernambuco state, known around the world for his work in experimental music and jazz. Winner of eight Grammy Awards.

Nara Leão

(1942-1989). Brazilian singer from Espírito Santo state who began her career in bossa nova before expanding to other genres and musical movements, including Tropicália and political song, including the show Opinião.

Nei Lopes

(1942-). Singer, composer, writer, and scholar of African diasporic culture. His books include *Dicionário da História Social do Samba* (2016, co-written with Luiz Antonio Simas) and *Enciclopédia Brasileira da Diáspora Africana* (2004).

Noel Rosa

(1910-1937). Singer and songwriter of classic sambas such as "Com que roupa?" and "Feitiço da Vila." His compositions chronicle the day to day life of bohemian Rio de Janeiro during the 1920s and 30s. Mandolin and guitar-player.

Oswald de Andrade

(1890-1954). Poet, essayist, and playwright from São Paulo. Central figure in the Brazilian modernist movement, one of the main figures in the 1922 "Modern Art Week" in São Paulo. Author of the famous "Brazil-Wood Manifesto" (1924) and "Cannibalist Manifesto" (1928).

Paschoal Carlos Magno
(1906-1980). Diplomat and theater critic, well-known for his writing on Brazilian theater.

Paulo Vanzolini
(1924-2013). Composer and zoologist, considered one of the major figures in samba from São Paulo. His songs include the classic "Ronda."

Paulo Villaça
(1933-1992). Brazilian actor, considered one of the main figures in the *cinema marginal* movement of the 1960s and 70s.

Pedro Loureiro
(n.d.). Singer and songwriter. Producer for Elza Soares.

Rafael Mike
(1979-). Songwriter, singer, dancer and cultural agitator from Rio de Janeiro.

Roberto Frejat
(1962-). Musician, songwriter and co-founder of the Brazilian rock band Barão Vermelho.

Roberto Menescal
(1937-). Musician and songwriter, born in Espírito Santo state. Considered a founding member of the bossa nova movement. His best-known songs include "O barquinho" and "Nós e o mar," composed with Ronaldo Bôscoli.

Roberto Ribeiro
(1940-1996). Singer and songwriter of samba and samba-enredo, born in Rio de Janeiro state.

Rodrigo Campos
(1977-). Songwriter, singer, and cavaquinho player from São Paulo.

Rômulo Fróes
(1971-). Songwriter, singer, and electric guitarist from São Paulo who played with the groups Passo Torto and Clube da Encruza.

Ronaldo Bôscoli
(1928-1994). Songwriter, music producer, and journalist from Rio de Janeiro. Composed the bossa nova standards "O barquinho" and "Nós e o mar" with Roberto Menescal.

Russo Passapusso
(1983-). Singer and songwriter from Bahia, vocalist for BaianaSystem, a group that fuses reggae, hip hop and samba from the region known as the Recôncavo Baiano.

Seu Jorge
(1970-). Jorge Mário da Silva. Singer, songwriter, multi-instrumentalist, and actor from Rio de Janeiro. Active in the genres of samba and MPB.

Simone Soul
(1970-). Percussionist from São Paulo who played with groups such as

Orquideas do Brasil and Funk Como Le Gusta.

Sylvinha Telles
(1934-1966). Singer and songwriter from Rio de Janeiro, considered a leading representative of bossa nova, despite the fact that her albums are out of print.

Tárik de Souza
(1946-). Journalist and music critic, considered a central figure in music criticism of *música popular brasileira* (MPB).

Tom Jobim
(1927-1996). Pianist, composer, and singer from Rio de Janeiro. Considered one of the co-founders of bossa nova.

Trio Mocotó
(1968-). Samba-rock ensemble that accompanied Jorge Benjor on many recordings, including the well-known "Que Pena" and "País Tropical."

Vinicius de Moraes
(1913-1980). Poet, diplomat, playwright, and composer from Rio de Janeiro. One of the central figures in 20th century Brazilian poetry and co-founder of the bossa nova genre.

Virgínia Rodrigues
(1964-). Singer from Bahia whose work fuses classical music, samba, and jazz.

Wilson das Neves
(1936-2017). Drummer, singer, and song-writer from Rio de Janeiro who accompanied artists such as Elis Regina, Roberto Carlos, Nara Leão, Elza Soares, Caetano Veloso, Gilberto Gil, Gal Costa, Chico Buarque, among others. One of his best-known songs is "O samba é meu dom."

Wilson Simonal
(1938-2000). Singer and songwriter from Rio de Janeiro, a leading figure in the 1960s and 70s samba soul movement. Named one of the best Brazilian singers of all time in 2012 by *Rolling Stone* magazine.

Zeca Pagodinho
(1959-). Singer and songwriter from Rio de Janeiro, one of the central figures in the genres of samba and pagode between 1980 and the present.

Zé Keti
(1921-1999). José Flores de Deus. Singer and songwriter of sambas, including the canonical "Eu Sou o Samba" and "Opinião."

Zé Rodrix
(1947-2009). José Rodrigues Trindade. Composer, Multi-instrumentalist, singer, and songwriter from Rio de Janeiro whose work spanned bossa nova, MPB, and rock.

DISCOGRAPHY

1960
SE ACASO VOCÊ CHEGASSE

Label: Odeon – MOFB-3166
Producer: Ismael Corrêa
Arrangement: Oswaldo Borba

SIDE A

1. Se Acaso Você Chegasse (F. Martins, Lupicínio Rodrigues)
2. Casa De Turfista... Cavalo De Pau (H. de Almeida, Macedo Netto)
3. Mulata Assanhada (Ataulfo Alves)
4. Era Bom (Hianto de Almeida, Macedo Netto)
5. Samba Em Copa (Cyro Monteiro)
6. Dedo Duro (Carlito, Zeca Do Pandeiro)

SIDE B

1. Teleco-Teco Nº 2 (Nelsinho, O. Magalhães)
2. Contas (Amâncio Cardoso)
3. Sal E Pimenta (N. de Brito, N. Ramalho)
4. Cartão De Visita (Edgardo Luis, N. Pereira De Castro)
5. Nêgo Tu...Nêgo Vós...Nêgo Você... (H. de Almeida, Macedo Netto)
6. Não Quero Mais (Astor, Julio Hungria)

1960
A BOSSA NEGRA

Label: Odeon – MOFB 3198
Producer: Ismael Corrêa
Arrangement: Astor Silva

SIDE A
1. Tenha Pena De Mim (Babaú, Ciro De Sousa)
2. Boato (João Roberto Kelly)
3. Fala Baixinho (Arcenio De Carvalho, Edson Menezes)
4. Marambaia (Henricão, Rubens Campos)
5. O Samba Está Com Tudo (Denis Brean, Oswaldo Guilherme)
6. Cadeira Vazia (Alcides Gonçalves, Lupicínio Rodrigues)

SIDE B
1. Perdão (Don Carlos, J. Assumpção)
2. Beija-Me (Mário Rossi, Roberto Martins)
3. O Bilhete (Dunga)
4. O Samba Brasileiro (Claribalte Passos)
5. As Polegadas Da Mulata (Hianto de Almeida, Macedo Neto)
6. Eu Quero É Sorongar (Candido Dias Da Cruz, Pedro Santos)

1961
O SAMBA É...

Label: Odeon – MOFB 3235
Producer: Ismael Corrêa
Arrangement: Astor Silva

SIDE A

1. Eu E O Rio (Luiz Antônio)
2. Vedete Certinha (Haroldo Barbosa, Luiz Reis)
3. Teleco-Teco (Marino Pinto, Murilo Caldas) with Monsueto Menezes
4. Bom Mesmo É Estar De Bem (Romeo Nunes, Silvio Silva)
5. Fez Bobagem (Assis Valente)
6. Amor De Mentira (Edson Borges, Hianto de Almeida)

SIDE B

1. Na Base Do Bilhetinho (Haroldo Barbosa, Luiz Reis)
2. Cantiga Do Morro (Hianto de Almeida, Macedo Neto) with Monsueto Menezes
3. Acho Que Sim (Antonio Carlos Jobim, Billy Blanco)
4. Ziriguidum (Monsueto Menezes) com Monsueto Menezes
5. Vou Sonhar Prá Você Ver (Haroldo Lobo, Milton de Oliveira)
6. Reconciliação (Marino Pinto, Waldemar Gomes)

1963
SAMBOSSA

Label: Odeon – MOFB-3296
Producer: José Ribamar
Direction: Milton Miranda

SIDE A

1. Rosa Morena (Dorival Caymmi)

2. Gamação (João Roberto Kelly)

3. A Banca Do Distinto (Billy Blanco)

4. Primeira Comunhão (Billy Blanco, Miguel Xavier)

5. Sim E Não (Carlos Magno, Edilton Lopes, Venâncio)

6. Leilão (Armando Nunes, Nazareno de Brito)

SIDE B

1. Só Danço Samba (Antonio Carlos Jobim, Vinicius De Moraes)

2. A Corda E A Caçamba (Antonio Almeida)

3. Vaca De Presépio (Billy Blanco)

4. Maria Mária Mariá (Billy Blanco)

5. Quando O Amor Não É Mais Amor (Cirene Mendonça, Ricardo Galeno)

6. Mulata De Verdade (Sergio Malta)

1964
NA RODA DO SAMBA

Label: Odeon – MOFB-3300
Producer: Milton Miranda
Musical Direction: Lyrio Panicali

SIDE A

1. Na Roda Do Samba (Orlandivo, Helton Menezes)
2. Dja Ba Dja (Lourenço Quintanilha, Izidro Quintanilha)
3. Convite Ao Samba (Osvaldo Guilherme, Denis Brean)
4. Na Base Do Pinguim (João Leal Brito 'Britinho', Fernando César)
5. Pressentimento (Osmar Navarro, Alcina Maria)
6. Samba Primeiro (Wilson Melo, Tony Martinelli)

SIDE B

1. Nêgo (Waldemar Gomes, Afonso Teixeira)
2. Gostoso É Sambar (João Mello)
3. Vou Rir De Você (Hélton Menezes)
4. Princesa Isabel (Sergio Ricardo)
5. Domingo Em Copacabana (Paulo Tito, Roberto Faissal)
6. Banca De Pobre (Rildo Hora, Marcos André)

1965
UM SHOW DE ELZA

Label: Odeon – MOFB-3420
Producer: Milton Miranda
Musical Direction: Lyrio Panicali
Arrangement: Maestro Nelsinho

SIDE A

1. Ocultei (Ary Barroso)
2. Verão No Meu Rio (Carla Baroni, Carlito)
3. Dindi (Aloysio De Oliveira, Antonio Carlos Jobim)
4. Samba Da Minha Terra (Dorival Caymmi)
5. Ombro A Ombro (Izidro Quintanilha, Lourenço Quintanilha)
6. Pé Redondo (Garrincha)

SIDE B

1. Vingança (Lupicínio Rodrigues)
2. Sambou Sambou (João Donato, João Mello)
3. Porque E Para Que (Fernando César, Jaime Florence "Meira")
4. Neném (Anselmo Mazzoni, Luis Bandeira)
5. Cais Do Porto (Capiba)
6. Se Acaso Você Chegasse (Felisberto Martins, Lupicínio Rodrigues)

1966
COM A BOLA BRANCA

Label: Odeon – MOFB-3459
Producer: Milton Miranda
Musical Direction: Lyrio Panicali
Arrangement: Maestro Nelsinho

SIDE A

1. Quizumba (Serrinha)
2. Estatuto Da Gafieira (Billy Blanco)
3. Nem Vem, Nem Vai (Synval Silva)
4. No Carnaval (Mendes)
5. Jogado Fora (João Mello)
6. A Vida Como Ela É (Júlio Dias de Castro)

SIDE B

1. A Infelicidade (Mauro Duarte, Niltinho)
2. Deixa A Nega Gingar (Luiz Claudio)
3. Brincadeira Tem Hora (Chico Feitosa, Mario Castro Neves)
4. Volta Pro Morro (Célio Cyrino, Manoel Ferreira)
5. Meu Tudo E Por Que (Carlito, Romeo Nunes)
6. Tudo É Balanço (Nilton Pereira, Niquinho)

1967
O MÁXIMO EM SAMBA

Label: Odeon – MOFB-3500
Producer: Milton Miranda
Musical Direction: Lyrio Panicali
Arrangement: Maestro Nelsinho

SIDE A

1. O Mundo Encantado De Monteiro Lobato (Batista Da Mangueira, Darcy, Luiz)
2. Conversa De Botequim (Noel Rosa, Vadico)
3. Tristeza (Haroldo Lôbo, Niltinho)
4. Agora É Cinza (Marçal, Bide)
5. Louco (Ela É O Seu Mundo) (Henrique De Almeida, Wilson Baptista)
6. O Orvalho Vem Caindo (Kid Pepe, Noel Rosa)

SIDE B

1. Atira A Primeira Pedra (Ataulpho Alves, Mário Lago)
2. Devagar Com A Louça (Haroldo Barbosa, Luiz Reis)
3. Vem Morar Comigo (Aldacir Louro, Eduardo Rocha, Fernando Martins)
4. Você Não Tem Palavra (Ataulpho Alves, Newton Teixeira)
5. Leva Meu Samba (Ataulpho Alves)
6. P'ra Machucar Meu Coração (Ary Barroso)

1967
ELZA, MILTINHO E SAMBA

Label: Odeon – MOFB-3510
Producer: Milton Miranda
Musical Direction: Lyrio Panicali
Arrangement: Maestro Nelsinho

SIDE A

1. Com Que Roupa (Noel Rosa) / Se Você Jurar (Francisco Alves, Ismael Silva, Nilton Bastos)
2. Beijo Na Bôca (Augusto Garcez, Cyro De Souza) / Moreninha Do Pom Pom Grená (Dorival Caymmi) / Tem Que Ter (Tulio Piva)
3. Boogie-Woogie Na Favela (Denis Brean) / Bonitão (Marino Pinto, Mário Rossi) / Eu Quero Um Samba (Haroldo Barbosa, Joel De Almeida) / Pourquoi (Essa Nêga Sem Sandália) (Caco Velho, Jadir De Castro)
4. Se Você Visse (Del Loro, Horondino Silva)
5. Todo Dia É Dia (Benedito Reis, Zuzuca 'Adil de Paula')

SIDE B

1. Enlouqueci (João Sale, Luiz Soberano, Waldomiro Pereira) / Fica Doido Varrido (Benedicto Lacerda, Frazão) / Obsessão (Milton de Oliveira, Mirabeau) / Só Eu Sei (Henrique De Almeida, Milton de Oliveira, Nelson Trigueiro) / É Bom Parar (Rubens Soares) / Calado Venci (Ataulpho Alves, Herivelto Martins) / Vai Que Depois Eu Vou (Adolfo Macêdo, Ayrton Borges, Zé Da Zilda) / Já Vai? (Duba, Rubens Campos)
2. Mal De Amor (Benil Santos, Raul Sampaio)
3. Antonico (Ismael Silva)
4. Louco De Saudade (Denis Brean)

1968
ELZA, MILTINHO E SAMBA 2

Label: Odeon – MOFB-3540
Producer: Milton Miranda
Musical Direction: Lyrio Panicali
Arrangement: Maestro Nelsinho

SIDE A

1. Dialogo De Criolos (Nelsinho)
2. Alô Alô (André Filho) / Pelo Telefone (Donga, Mauro de Almeida)
3. Semana Inteira (Roberto Carlos, Erasmo Carlos) / O Pau Comeu Na Casa De Noca (Catulo de Paula)
4. Vaidosa (Herivelto Martins, Arthur Morais) / Me Deixa Em Paz (Herivelto Martins, Jovelino Marques da Costa) / Para Me Livrar Do Mal (Noel Rosa, Ismael Silva)
5. Tenha Pena De Mim (Ciro de Souza, Kid Pepe)

SIDE B

1. Você Jà Foi À Bahia? (Dorival Caymmi) / Vestido De Bolero (Dorival Caymmi)
2. Mancada (Gilberto Gil) / Vai Haver Barulho No Château (Valfrido Silva, Noel Rosa)
3. Promessa (Jaime de Carvalho "Colô") / Confesso (Ivone Lara) / Quem Chorou Fui Eu (Haroldo Lobo, Milton Oliveira)
4. Pot Pourri De Imitação

1968
ELZA SOARES
BATERISTA: WILSON DAS NEVES

Label: Odeon – MOFB-3521
Producer: Milton Miranda
Musical Direction: Lyrio Panicali
Arrangement: Maestro Nelsinho

SIDE A

1. Balanço Zona Sul (Tito Madi)
2. Deixa Isso Prá La (Alberto Paz, Edson Menezes)
3. Garota De Ipanema (Antonio Carlos Jobim, Vinicius De Moraes)
4. Edmundo = In The Mood (Aloysio De Oliveira, Andy Razaf, Joe Garland)
5. O Pato (Jayme Silva, Neuza Teixeira)
6. Copacabana (Alberto Ribeiro, João De Barro)

SIDE B

1. Teleco Teco Nº 2 (Nelsinho, Oldemar Magalhães)
2. Saudade Da Bahia (Dorival Caymmi)
3. Samba De Verão (Marcos Valle, Paulo Sérgio Valle)
4. Se Acaso Você Chegasse (Felisberto Martins, Lupicínio Rodrigues)
5. Mulata Assanhada (Ataulfo Alves)
6. Palhaçada (Haroldo Barbosa, Luiz Reis)

1969
ELZA, CARNAVAL & SAMBA

Label: Odeon – MOFB-3589
Producer: Milton Miranda
Musical Direction: Lyrio Panicali
Arrangement: Maestro Nelsinho

SIDE A
1. Bahia de Todos Os Deuses (Salgueiro - Samba-Enredo 1969) (Bala, Manoel Rosa)
2. Quero Morrer no Carnaval (Luiz Antônio, Eurico Campos)
3. Não Me Diga Adeus (Paquito, Luis Soberano, João Correia da Silva)
4. Eu Chorarei Amanhã (Raul Sampaio, Ivo Santos)
5. De Lanterna na Mão (Elzo Augusto, José Saccomani, Jorge Martins)
6. Fechei A Porta (Sebastião Mota, Ferreira dos Santos)

SIDE B
1. Heróis da Liberdade (Império Serrano - Samba-Enredo 1969) (Silas de Oliveira, Mano Décio da Viola, Manoel Ferreira)
2. Rosa Maria (Aníbal Silva, Eden Silva)
3. Eu Agora Sou Feliz (José Bispo 'Jamelão', Mestre Gato)
4. Que Samba Bom (Geraldo Pereira, Arnaldo Passos)
5. Falam de Mim (Noel Rosa de Oliveira, Eden Silva, Aníbal Silva)
6. Se É Pecado Sambar (Manoel Santana)

1969
ELZA, MILTINHO E SAMBA 3

Label: Odeon – MOFB-3604
Producer: Milton Miranda
Musical Direction: Lyrio Panicali
Arrangement: Maestro Nelsinho

SIDE A

1. Juntinhos de Novo (Nelsinho) / Não Manche o Meu Panamá (Alcebíades Nogueira) / O Sorriso do Paulinho (Gastão Viana, Mário Rossi) / Oito Mulheres (José Batista) / Embrulho Que Eu Carrego (Alvaiade, Djalma Mafra) / Despacho (Ary Barroso)
2. Saia do Caminho (Custódio Mesquita, Evaldo Ruy) / Nervos de Aço (Lupicínio Rodrigues) / Por Causa de Você (Tom Jobim, Dolores Duran)
3. Só Com Você (Anselmo Mazzoni)
4. Julgar É Missão Divina (João Machado, Hélio Simões)

SIDE B

1. Vai na Paz de Deus (Ataulfo Alves, Antônio Domingues) / Conceição (Octaciliano Silveira, Chiquinho Storino) / Aos Pés da Cruz (Marino Pinto, Zé da Zilda) / Se a Saudade Me Apertar (Ataulfo Alves, Jorge de Castro) / Você Não Quer Nem Eu (Ataulfo Alves)
2. Com Olhos de Gata (João Pereira da Fonseca) / Fita Amarela (Noel Rosa) / Madeira de Lei (Luiz Bandeira, Renato Araújo)
3. Samba Da Cor (Castrinho, Marli De Oliveira)
4. Madrugada Vai Chegar (David Correia)
5. Um Samba Pra Ela (Benil Santos, José Orlando)

1970
SAMBAS & MAIS SAMBAS

Label: Odeon – MOFB-3646
Producer: Milton Miranda
Musical Direction: Lyrio Panicali
Arrangement: Maestro Nelsinho

SIDE A
1. Mas Que Nada (Jorge Ben)
2. Recado (Paulinho da Viola, Casquinha)
3. Dá-me Tuas Mãos (Erasmo Silva, Jorge de Castro)
4. Vejam Só (Getúlio Macedo)
5. Pressentimento (Élton Medeiros, Hermínio Bello de Carvalho)
6. Máscara da Face (Klécius Caldas, Armando Cavalcanti)

SIDE B
1. Tributo a Martin Luther King (Wilson Simonal, Ronaldo Bôscoli)
2. Comunicação (Chico Feitosa, Marcello Silva)
3. Maior É Deus (Felisberto Martins, Fernando Martins)
4. Tributo A Dom Fuas (Carlos Imperial, Fernando César)
5. Seu José (Silvio César)
6. Meu Consolo É Você (Antônio Nássara, Roberto Martins)

1972
SANGUE, SUOR E RAÇA (WITH ROBERTO RIBEIRO)

Label: Odeon – MOFB-3752
Producer: Milton Miranda
Assistant: Hermínio Bello de Carvalho
Arrangement: Dom Salvador

SIDE A

1. Swing Negrão (Elza Soares) / Brasil Pandeiro (Assis Valente) / O Samba Agora Vai (Pedro Caetano) / É Com Esse Que Eu Vou (Pedro Caetano)
2. Aurora de Um Sambista (Toco)
3. Domingos, Domingueira (Eduardo Marques)
4. Cicatrizes (Miltinho "MPB-4", Paulo César Pinheiro)
5. Isto É Papel, João (Paulo Rushell) / Cocorocó (Paulo da Portela) / Decadência (Cartola)

SIDE B

1. Recordação de Um Batuqueiro (Xangô da Mangueira, J. Gomes)
2. O Que Vem de Baixo Não Me Atinge (Johnny Alf)
3. Lenço Cor de Rosa (Eduardo Marques)
4. Sacrifício (Mauro Duarte, Maurício Tapajós)
5. Coisa Louca (Ismael Silva) / A Razão Dá-se A Quem Tem (Francisco Alves, Noel Rosa, Ismael Silva) / O Que Se Leva Dessa Vida (Pedro Caetano)

1972

ELZA PEDE PASSAGEM

Label: Odeon – MOFB-3711
Producer: Milton Miranda
Arrangement: Lyndolfo Gaya

SIDE A

1. Cheguendengo (Antônio Carlos Pinto, Jocafi, Renato Luis Lobo)
2. Saltei de Banda (Zé Rodrix, Luiz Carlos Sá)
3. Maria Vai Com As Outras (Toquinho, Vinicius de Moraes)
4. Samba da Pá (João Só)
5. Abc da Vida (Luiz Reis, Haroldo Barbosa)
6. Barão Beleza (Tuzé de Abreu)

SIDE B

1. Rio Carnaval dos Carnavais (Padeirinho, Nilton Russo, Moacir)
2. O Gato (Gonzaguinha)
3. Pulo Pulo (Jorge Ben)
4. Amor Perfeito (Billy Blanco)
5. Mais do Que Eu (João Nogueira)

1973
ELZA SOARES

Label: Odeon – MOFB-3817
Producer: Milton Miranda
Musical Direction: Lyndolfo Gaya
Arrangement: Laércio de Freitas

SIDE A

1. Eu Não Toco Berimbau (Serrinha, Mazola)
2. Busto Calado (Rubens Silva, Orlando Costa 'Maestro Cipó')
3. Pranto de Poeta (Nelson Cavaquinho, Guilherme de Brito)
4. Dia De Graça (Candeia)
5. Maria José (Fritz, Nereu Gargalo)
6. Zelão (Sérgio Ricardo)

SIDE B

1. Canoa Furada (Gisa Nogueira)
2. Solidão (Luiz Roberto, Paulo Martini)
3. Sete Linhas (Sidney da Conceição)
4. Festa da Vinda (Cartola, Nuno Veloso)
5. Lá Vou Eu (Délcio Carvalho)
6. Aquarela Brasileira (Silas de Oliveira)

1974
ELZA SOARES

Label: Tapecar - LPX23
Producer: Ismael Corrêa
Arrangement: Ed Lincoln

SIDE A
1. Bom Dia Portela (David Correia, Bebeto Di São João)
2. Pranto Livre (Dida, Everaldo da Viola)
3. Não É Hora de Tristeza (Lino Roberto, Wilson Medeiros, Walter da Imperatriz)
4. Meia-Noite Já É Dia (Norival Reis, David Correia)
5. Desabafo (Tatu, Nezinho, Campo)
6. Partido do Lê Lê Lê (Otilo Gomes)

SIDE B
1. Deusa do Rio Niger (Walter Norambê, Motorzinho)
2. Quem Há de Dizer (Lupicínio Rodrigues, Alcides Gonçalves)
3. Louvei Maria (Elza Soares)
4. Xamêgo de Crioula (Zé Di)
5. Falso Papel (Dário Marciano)
6. Giringonça (Josealdo Fraga)

1975
NOS BRAÇOS DO SAMBA

Label: Tapecar - LPX34
Producer: Ed Lincoln

SIDE A

1. Primeiro Eu (Romildo Bastos, Toninho Nascimento)
2. Nem Vem (Levo Minha Viola) (Noel Rosa de Oliveira, Duduca, José Alves)
3. Viagem de Jangada (Tião da Roça, Antônio Andrade)
4. Quem É Bom Já Nasce Feito (Lino Roberto, Wilson Medeiros)
5. Debruçado Em Meu Olhar (Romildo Bastos, Toninho Nascimento)
6. Confesso Que Chorei (João Fonseca, Albano Silva)

SIDE B

1. Lendas e Festas das Yabás (União da Ilha do Governador
- Samba-enredo 1974)
(Aroldo Melodia, Leôncio da Silva)
2. Nos Braços do Samba (Neoci, Dida)
3. Auera (Marcos Moran, E. Carlos)
4. Saudade Minha Inimiga (Nelson Cavaquinho, Guilherme de Brito)
5. Deixa Pra Deus Resolver (Gilson de Souza)
6. Cansada de Esperar (Ciro Vagareza, Sidney da Conceição)

1976
LIÇÃO DE VIDA

Label: Tapecar - LPX42
Producer: Ed Lincoln
Arrangement: Paulo Moura

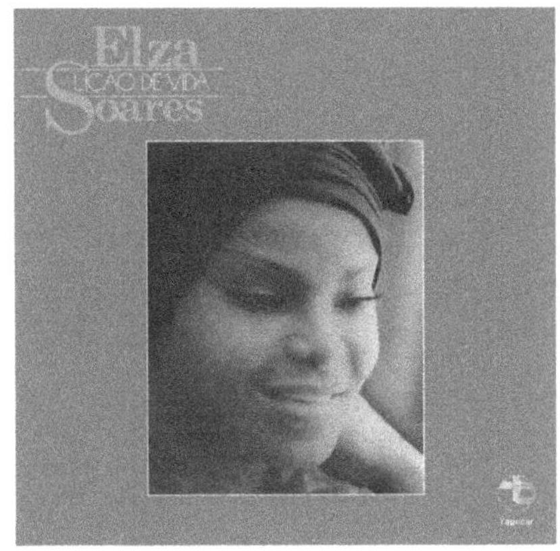

SIDE A
1. Malandro (Jorge Aragão, Jotabê)
2. Cipriano (Sidney da Conceição, Romeo Nunes)
3. Lição de Vida (Paulo de Capitólia)
4. Pinta e Borda (Belizário, Di Ferraz)
5. Rainha dos Sete Mares (Avarese, Lino Roberto, Alfredo Silva)
6. A Rosa (Efson)

SIDE B
1. Curumbandê (Beto Baiano)
2. Nó Na Tristeza (Vicente Matos, Carlito Cavalcanti)
3. Deus e Viola (Neoci, Dida)
4. Estou Com Raiva de Você (Miro Barbosa, Jorge Roberto)
5. Samba Minha Raiz (Dona Ivone Lara, Délcio Carvalho)
6. Sal e Pimenta (Nazareno de Brito, Newton Ramalho) / Mulata Assanhada (Ataulfo Alves) / Beija-me (Roberto Martins, Mário Rossi)

1977
PILÃO + RAÇA = ELZA

Label: Tapecar - LPX47
Producer: Gilson Paranzetta

SIDE A

1. Língua de Pilão (Elza Soares)
2. Enredo de Pirraça (Elza Soares, Gerson Alves)
3. Aldeia de Okarimbé (Aloísio, César Veneno/Naval)
4. Sombra Confidente (Gerson Alves)
5. Perdão Vila Isabel (Elza Soares, Gerson Alves)
6. Perdão Amor (Jorge Aragão, Neoci)

SIDE B

1. De Pandeiro na Mão (João Roberto Kelly)
2. Só Tem Um Jeito Agora (Roberto Neves)
3. Amor Aventureiro (Mano Décio da Viola, Silas de Oliveira)
4. Compositor (Rildo Hora, Sérgio Cabral)
5. Prezado Amigo (Rildo Hora, Sérgio Cabral)
6. Só Uma Lágrima (Acyr Pimentel)

1979
SENHORA DA TERRA

Label: CBS 138160
Producer: Maestro Nelsinho

SIDE A

1. Põe Pimenta (Beto Sem Braço, Jorginho Saberás)
2. Coração Vadio (Edil Pacheco, Paulinho Diniz)
3. O Morro (Mauro Duarte, Dona Ivone Lara)
4. Exaltação ao Rio São Francisco (Waltinho, Zezé do Pandeiro, João Leonel)
5. Afoxé (Heraldo Farias, João Belém)
6. Maria Pequena (Guaracy de Castro, Roberto Nepomuceno)

SIDE B

1. Abertura (Elza Soares)
2. Alegria do Povo (Luis Luz, Ari do Cavaco)
3. O Carnaval (Gerson Alves, Valentim)
4. Vê Só Malandragem (Valentim, Gerson Alves)
5. Paródia do Consumidor (Nei Lopes, Wilson Moreira)
6. Barraquinho (João Roberto Kelly)

1980
NEGRA ELZA, ELZA NEGRA

Label: CBS 138084
Producer: João de Aquino

SIDE A

1. Como Lutei (Wilson Moreira/Nei Lopes)
2. Cobra Cainana (João de Aquino/Hermínio Bello de Carvalho)
3. Timbó (Ramon Russo)
4. O Porteiro Me Enganou (Haroldo Lobo/Milton de Oliveira)
5. Oração de Duas Raças (Gerson Alves)

SIDE B

1. Artimanha (Gerson Alves)
2. Olindina (Tião Valentim/Antônio Valentim)
3. Fim de Noite (Chico Feitosa/Ronaldo Bôscoli)
4. É Isso Aí (Betinho/Marco Antônio Rosa)
5. Samba do Mirerê (Tradicional/Adpt. Gerson Alves)
6. Capitão do Mato (Gerson Alves)

1985
SOMOS TODOS IGUAIS

Label: Som Livre - 530017
Producer: Glaucus Xavier
Artistic Direction: Max Pierre

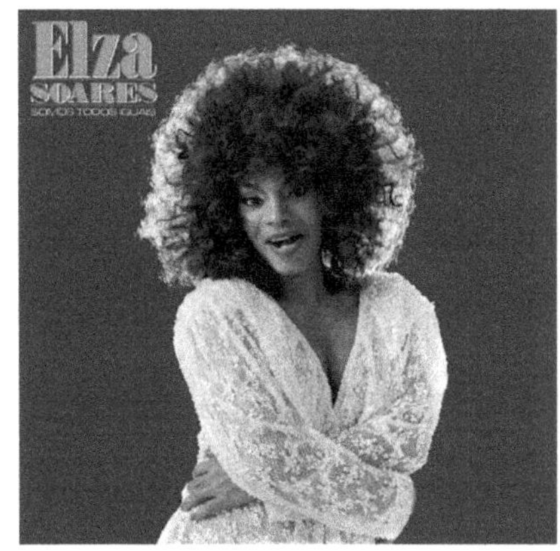

SIDE A

1. Osso, Pele E Pano (Jorge Aragão)
2. Mais Uma Vez (Carlos Dafé, Lourenço)
3. Da Fuga Fez Sua Verdade (Adilson Victor, Sereno, Sombrinha)
4. Cacatua (Ronaldo Barcellos)
5. Daquele Amor, Nem Me Fale (João Donato, Martinho da Vila)
6. Heróis da Liberdade (Império Serrano - Samba-Enredo 1969) (Silas de Oliveira, Mano Décio da Viola, Manoel Ferreira)

SIDE B

1. Somos Todos Iguais (Elza Soares)
2. Antes do Sol (Ronaldo Barcellos, Pi)
3. Sophisticated Lady (Irving Mills, Mitchell Parish, Duke Ellington, Adapt. Augusto de Campos). Featuring: Caetano Veloso
4. Exagero (Elza Soares, Glaucus Xavier)
5. Milagres (Roberto Frejat, Denise Barros, Cazuza)

1988
VOLTEI

Label: RGE 303.6120
Producer: Milton Manhães

SIDE A

1. Voltei (Oswaldo Nunes, Celso Castro) / Bom Dia Portela (David Correia, Bebeto Di São João) / Malandro (Jorge Aragão, Jotabê)
2. Doce Acalanto (Noca da Portela, Nelson Rufino)
3. Amor Sublime (Noca da Portela, Sereno, Roberto Serrão)
4. Plenitude (Pedrinho da Flor, Fernando Baster)
5. Erê (Beto Sem Braço, Bandeira Brasil)

SIDE B

1. Lá Vem Você (Wilson Ney)
2. Sem Ilusão (Paulo Santana, Jorge Santana, Carzé)
3. Ânsia Louca (Adilson Bispo, Zé Roberto)
4. Coisas da Gente (Sombrinha, Arlindo Cruz, Luiz Carlos da Vila)
5. Nesse Trem (Paulo Santana, Jorge Santana, Carzé)

1997
TRAJETÓRIA

Label: Universal Music UMD
51020
Producer: José Milton
Artistic Direction:
Sérgio de Carvalho

1. Rio de Janeiro (Guinga/Aldir Blanc)
2. Estou Lhe Devendo Um Sorriso (Serafim Adriano)
3. Sinhá Mandaçaia (Almir Guineto, Luverci Ernesto)
Featuring: Zeca Pagodinho
4. Bom Dia (Herivelto Martins, Aldo Cabral)
5. Justa Causa (Noca da Portela, Toninho Nascimento)
6. Dói Demais (Everaldo Cruz, Nei Lopes)
7. Boato (João Roberto Kelly)
8. Trajetória (Arlindo Cruz, Serginho Meriti, Franco)
9. Lá No Alto Da Colina (Domenil)
10. Liberdade Para Amar (Elza Soares, Iberê Melodia)
11. Chuvas de Verão (Fernando Lobo)
12. Cuidado, Mané (Luiz Grande, Ari do Cavaco)
13. Mais Uma Ilusão (Alvinho Santos, Beto Menezes)
14. O Meu Guri (Chico Buarque)

1999
**CARIOCA DA GEMA -
ELZA AO VIVO**

Label: Luna 5122096
**Recorded live in
Rio de Janeiro
April 1999**

1. Lata D'Água (Elza Soares)
2. Balanço Zona Sul (Tito Madi)
3. Malandro (Jorge Aragão, Jotabê)
4. Lobo Bobo (Carlos Lyra, Ronaldo Bôscoli)
5. Quatro Loucos Num Samba (Cyro Monteiro, Mary Monteiro)
6. Cadeira Vazia (Lupicínio Rodrigues, Alcides Gonçalves)
7. Antonico (Ismael Silva)
8. Castigo (Dolores Duran)
9. Circo Marimbondo (Milton Nascimento, Ronaldo Bastos)
10. Chove Chuva (Jorge Ben Jor)
11. O Dono Da Terra (Carlinhos Melodia, Haroldo Pereira, Vicente das Neves, Alexandre Alegria, Rono Maia)
12. Desde Que O Samba É Samba (Caetano Veloso)
13. Trem das Onze (Adoniran Barbosa)
14. Pot-pourri "Turma Da Pilantragem": País Tropical (Jorge Ben Jor) / Meu Limão, Meu Limoeiro (Tradicional/Adpt. José Carlos Burle) / Mamãe Passou Açúcar Em Mim (Carlos Imperial)
15. Hino Nacional Brasileiro (Francisco Manoel da Silva, Joaquim Osório Duque Estrada)

2002

DO CÓCCIX ATÉ O PESCOÇO

Label: Maianga Discos
Catalogue: 789836945 001 6
Producer: José Miguel Wisnik
Arrangement: Alê Siqueira

1. Dura Na Queda (Chico Buarque)
2. Hoje É Dia De Festa (Jorge Ben Jor)
3. Haiti (Gilberto Gil/Caetano Veloso)
4. Dor de Cotovelo (Caetano Veloso)
5. Bambino (Ernesto Nazareth/Adpt. José Miguel Wisnik)
6. A Carne (Seu Jorge/Marcelo Yuka/Ulisses Cappelletti)
7. Eu Vou Ficar Aqui (Arnaldo Antunes). Featuring: Funk Como Le Gusta
8. Etnocopop (Carlinhos Brown)
9. Fadas (Luiz Melodia)
10. Flores Horizontais (Oswald de Andrade/José Miguel Wisnik)
11. A Cigarra (Elza Soares/Letícia Sabatella). Featuring: Letícia Sabatella
12. Pot-pourri "Quebra Lá Que Eu Quebro C"
13. Todo Dia (ABM de Aguiar)
14. Façamos (Vamos Amar) (Let's Do It) (Let's Fall In Love)
(Cole Porter/Adpt. Carlos Rennó). Featuring: Chico Buarque

2003
VIVO FELIZ

Label: Reco-Head Records
RH0007
Producer: Guilherme Mendonça

1. Intro
2. Opinião (Zé Keti)
3. Eu Gosto da Minha Terra (Randoval Montenegro)
4. Rio De Janeiro (Anderson Lugão)
5. Volta Por Cima (Paulo Vanzolini)
6. Somos Todos Iguais (Elza Soares)
7. Two Tac (Anderson Lugão)
8. Concórdia (Nando Reis)
9. Computadores Fazem Arte (Fred 04)
10. Lata D'Água (Elza Soares)

2007
BEBA-ME
ELZA SOARES AO VIVO

Label: Biscoito Fino BF 806
Recorded live at
Sesc Vila Mariana (SP)
March 2007

1. Meu Guri (Chico Buarque)
2. Beija-me (Roberto Martins, Mário Rossi)
3. Estatutos de Gafieira (Billy Blanco)
4. O Neguinho E A Senhorita (Noel Rosa de Oliveira, Abelardo da Silva)
5. Pra Que Discutir Com Madame (Haroldo Barbosa, Janet de Almeida)
6. Exagero (Elza Soares, Glaucus Xavier)
7. Dor de Cotovelo (Caetano Veloso)
8. Pranto Livre (Dida, Everaldo da Viola)
9. Palmas No Portão (Walter Dionisio, D'Acri Luis)
10. Lata D'Água (Luiz Antônio, Jota Júnior)
11. Teleco-Teco (Murilo Caldas, Marino Pinto)
12. Cartão de Visita (Edgardo Luis, Nilton Pereira de Castro)
13. Teleco-teco N° 2 (Nelsinho, Oldemar Magalhães)
14. Malandro (Jorge Aragão, Jotabê)
15. Rap da Felicidade (Julinho Rasta, Kátia)

2015
A MULHER DO FIM DO MUNDO

Label: Circus CPF 017
Producer: Guilherme Kastrup

SIDE A
1. Coração do Mar (José Miguel Wisnik, Oswald de Andrade)
2. A Mulher do Fim do Mundo (Rômulo Fróes, Alice Coutinho)
3. Maria da Vila Matilde (Douglas Germano)
4. Luz Vermelha (Kiko Dinucci, Clima)
5. Pra Fuder (Kiko Dinucci)
6. Firmeza?! (Rodrigo Campos). Featuring: Rodrigo Campos

SIDE B
1. Benedita (Celso Sim, Pepê Mata Machado, Joana Barossi, Fernanda Diamant). Featuring: Celso Sim
2. Dança (Rômulo Fróes, Cacá Machado). Featuring: Rômulo Fróes
3. O Canal (Rodrigo Campos)
4. Solto (Marcelo Cabral, Clima)
5. Comigo (Rômulo Fróes, Alberto Tassinari)

2018
DEUS É MULHER

Label: Deckdisc 22267-2
Producer: Guilherme Kastrup

1. O Que Se Cala (Douglas Germano)
2. Exu Nas Escolas (Kiko Dinucci, Edgar). Featuring: Edgar
3. Banho (Tulipa Ruiz)
4. Eu Quero Comer Você (Rômulo Fróes, Alice Coutinho)
5. Língua Solta (Rômulo Fróes, Alice Coutinho)
6. Hienas Na TV (Kiko Dinucci, Clima)
7. Clareza (Rodrigo Campos)
8. Um Olho Aberto (Mariá Portugal)
9. Credo (Douglas Germano)
10. Dentro de Cada Um (Luciano Mello, Pedro Loureiro).
Featuring: Bloco Afro Ilú Obá De Min
11. Deus Há De Ser (Pedro Luís)

2019
PLANETA FOME

Label: Deckdisc
Producer: Rafael Ramos

1. Libertação (Russo Passapusso).
Featuring: BaianaSystem and Virgínia Rodrigues
2. Menino (Elza Soares)
3. Brasis (Gabriel Moura, Seu Jorge, Jovi Joviniano)
4. Blá Blá Blá (Pedro Loureiro).
Featuring: BNegão and Pedro Loureiro
5. Comportamento Geral (Gonzaguinha)
6. Tradição (Sérgio Britto, Paulo Miklos)
7. Lírio Rosa (Luciano Mello, Pedro Loureiro)
8. Não Tá Mais de Graça (Rafael Mike).
Featuring: Rafael Mike
9. País do Sonho (Chapinha da Vela, Carlinhos Palhano)
10. Pequena Memória Para Um Tempo Sem Memória (A Legião
dos Esquecidos) (Gonzaguinha)
1. Virei o Jogo (Pedro Luís)
12. Não Recomendado (Caio Prado)

2021
ELZA SOARES
& JOÃO DE AQUINO

Label: Deckdisc
Recorded in one session at
Estúdio Haras, 1997

1. Drão (Gilberto Gil)
2. Canário Da Terra (João de Aquino, Aldir Blanc)
3. Hoje (Taiguara)
4. Devagar Com a Louça (Haroldo Barbosa, Luiz Reis)
5. Super-Homem (A Canção) (Gilberto Gil)
6. Antonico (Ismael Silva)
7. Meu Guri (Chico Buarque)
8. Mambo da Cantareira (Barbosa da Silva, Eloide Warthon)
9. Juventude Transviada (Luiz Melodia)
10. Eu Sonhei Que Tu Estavas Tão Linda (Lamartine Babo, Francisco Matoso)
11. Que Maravilha (Jorge Ben Jor, Toquinho)
12. Como Uma Onda (Zen Surfismo) (Lulu Santos, Nelson Motta)
13. Cartão de Visita (Edgardo Luis, Nilton Pereira de Castro)

THE
INVISIBLE
BRIDGE

The Invisible Bridge is a collective of publishers from different languages and locations - Backlands Press (English), Ediciones Andantes (Spanish), Les Mots Mobiles (French) and Oca Editorial (Portuguese) - with the purpose of establishing a permanent dialog between the cultures and thinking of these countries, with special attention to the production of the Global South. The proposal is to expand bibliodiversity, through books created especially for the publishers, with the concern of working with four fundamental axes: mapping cultural and scientific production, presenting it to a broad and non-specialized audience, reflecting on this production and stimulating creation. Made up of publishers, artists, researchers and translators from different areas and nationalities, the Invisible Bridge collective aims to be more than publishers, bridges between cultures.

www.ingramcontent.com/pod-product-compliance
Lightning Source LLC
Chambersburg PA
CBHW041840110726
48006CB00020B/2685